COLOMBIA
Portrait of
Unity and Diversity

COLOMBIA

Portrait of
Unity and Diversity

Harvey F. Kline

Westview Press / Boulder, Colorado

Westview Profiles / Nations of Contemporary Latin America

All photographs, except for 1.9 and 1.11 (which were supplied by the author), are courtesy of the Colombia Information Service. The three jacket photos show: (*upper left*) *campesino* children in Boyacá; (*upper right*) coffee growing in Andean Colombia; (*bottom*) Bogotá, the capital and largest city.

Published in 1983 in the United States of America by
Westview Press, Inc.
5500 Central Avenue
Boulder, Colorado 80301
Frederick A. Praeger, President and Publisher

Library of Congress Cataloging in Publication Data
Kline, Harvey F.
  Colombia.
  (Nations of contemporary Latin America)
  Bibliography: p.
  1. Colombia. I. Title. II. Series.
F2258.K55 1983   986.1   82-21926
ISBN 0-89158-941-4

Printed and bound in the United States of America

To my parents,
whose love and care made so many things possible,
and to the people of Colombia—
pueblo, oligarquía, and everyone in between—
con mi humilde deseo de un mejor porvenir.

Contents

Tables and Figures

Foreword

Colombia is perhaps the least well known or understood of the major countries of Latin America. With 28 million inhabitants, Colombia ranks third, with Argentina, in population—behind Brazil and Mexico. Nevertheless, it generally receives less attention in the United States and Europe than does its much smaller neighbor Venezuela. Although it is the world's second largest producer of coffee, Colombia is overshadowed by Brazil. Yet Colombians constitute an important and rapidly growing portion of the Latin American community in New York City. As indicated by President Reagan's recent trip, the country is likely to become less marginal to U.S. policy because of the large volume of illegal drugs that comes to the United States from—or at least through—Colombia. From a comparative perspective, Colombia merits attention as a country that is both Andean and Caribbean, although it lacks the large Indian population of other Andean countries and the heavy African influence more typical of the Caribbean.

Harvey Kline has provided a coherent picture of modern Colombia, its past, and its possible future. He has approached this rather difficult country in a balanced manner, neither dramatizing nor neglecting those aspects of its national life that have been brought to the world's attention by the highly political and deeply moving novels of Nobel Laureate Gabriel García Márquez, probably Colombia's most famous living national. Disdaining a rigid analytical framework, Professor Kline sticks to the essentials, providing readers with just enough information to gain an appreciation of this northernmost of South American countries without burdening them with superfluous details. As other authors in this series have done, Professor Kline uses photographs to complement his words, vividly illustrating the varied aspects of Colombian reality, from the pleasant and colorful to the grim and depressing.

International factors and foreign policy have been stressed less here than they have been in other volumes in this series. This reflects

Colombia's remarkably limited role in Inter-American affairs and its low visibility on the larger international scene—a relatively recent development. During the colonial period and through the nineteenth century, Colombia participated in nearly all of the significant movements that swept Latin America. Having long possessed one of the world's most strategic interoceanic and intercontinental links, the Isthmus of Panama, Colombia was abruptly deprived of this key economic and geopolitical asset by the United States just after the turn of the century. Weakened by a protracted and bloody civil war, Colombia could not respond effectively.

By the time Colombia recovered from the loss of its most valuable province, the great interwar depression had made economic survival the principal national concern; World War II was followed almost immediately by a decade of rampant violence. After it had taken at least 300,000 lives, *La Violencia* was finally ended by the establishment of a military dictatorship. The small degree of democracy reestablished after 1957 involved a rigid monopoly on elective office by two traditional parties, which drove newer political movements toward insurgency and terrorism. The memories of sociopolitical trauma are very much a part of the psychological make-up of Colombians of all ages.

In *Colombia* Professor Kline has wisely eschewed overly sophisticated and complex analysis, relying instead upon clear descriptions and incisive explanations. The result is a book that will greatly aid readers in understanding the problems facing Colombia in the 1980s and their implications for the world.

Ronald Schneider

Preface

Colombia, perhaps more than any other country in Latin America, has always frustrated those outsiders who try to understand and explain it. Marxists are frustrated by the lack of social class conflict. Liberal democrats don't understand why a country that has so many of the trappings of liberal democracy often does not act like one. Students of Latin American politics, expecting a praetorian state like those of the Southern Cone, do not find the military in power. Others, with the ideas of the cultural fragment of corporatism brought by the Spanish to the New World, find that fragment weak or nonexistent. If it is any consolation, Colombians themselves also are frustrated in explaining their country—and indeed fall into the above categories at different times.

In this book I attempt to describe the basic characteristics of this third most populous country south of the Rio Grande. Several general themes are important throughout: that we must do all possible to put preconceptions aside and allow Colombia to speak for itself; that the 28 million people of the country face incredible, and perhaps increasing, problems of living in an underdeveloped, Third World, or less developed country; and that, in some ways, Colombia does not exist, except in popular myth, academic reification, and in the assemblies of international organizations. Because of this last theme—the great diversity of the country—I thought of using the metaphor of a collage in the subtitle of this book. While in the end that metaphor was not used, it is still my belief that the country is a kind of multidimensional collage, approaching the surrealistic at times, in which all kinds of people are pasted together in incongruous relationships.

Developing this theme, the book begins with a description of the land and its people, followed by two chapters on the history of the country. Later chapters consider government and politics, the economic system and public policy issues, and international relations. Quite naturally, the book concludes with some speculations about the future.

Several things have frustrated me as I have written these pages. One is that the constraints of length have prevented me from adding detail at many places. Another is that, in the end, I cannot explain why Colombia has such an eclectic system. And finally I must admit candidly that there is no easy scapegoat for Colombia's problems. At the time that I was writing the first draft of these pages, I was reading Tom Walker's *Nicaragua: The Land of Sandino*. At times I found myself thinking, "If Colombia only had a Somoza on whom I could heap all blame!" I am not at all certain that Colombians would agree with that selfish wish on my part.

I hope that these pages, if nothing else, will allow people who have never spent time in Colombia to better understand the country, its promises, and its problems. If, at the end, the reader realizes that Colombia is more than Juan Valdés–like coffee growers and drug runners (although both of those kinds of people surely exist), then my work has not been in vain.

I would be remiss, finally, if I did not thank those who have made this project possible. During my four trips to Colombia (where I have had the good fortune to live for almost four years out of the last eighteen), literally hundreds of people have helped me in my attempts to understand, although perhaps they didn't realize that they were doing so. Space allows me to mention only a few: the Fulbright-Hayes Commission (which funded two research trips and was especially helpful during the latter thanks to its director, Francisco Gnecco Calvo), Latin American Teaching Fellowships, the Research Council of the University of Massachusetts/Amherst, and the people of the University of North Carolina/Chapel Hill who introduced me to Colombia by sending me there on an undergraduate exchange in 1964; the scores of Colombian politicians who have given me time over the years; and, most especially, my colleagues and good friends in the Departamento de Ciencia Política at the Universidad de los Andes, who, on three occasions, have been patient with me and generous with their assistance. In particular, Francisco Leal and Dora Rothlisberger (colleagues on three occasions) and Gabriel Murillo (my student the first time, colleague the second, and chairman the third) have contributed greatly to this book and richly deserve much of the praise for whatever merit this work might have.

I would like to thank also those people in the United States who read earlier versions of this manuscript, whose comments helped to make it better: Daniel Premo of Washington College, who commented on the entire manuscript; Jonathan Hartlyn of Vanderbilt, who made invaluable suggestions for Chapter 4; Edward Epstein of the University of Utah, whose advice helped greatly in improving Chapter 5; and Ronald Schneider, general editor of the Westview Profiles of Nations of Contemporary Latin America series, whom it was a great pleasure to have as editor. Mary Root also contributed, through her prompt and efficient typing of two versions of the manuscript, as did Winston Averill, who drafted the map.

Special appreciation goes to my wife, Dottie, who not only spent three years in Colombia with me but also was a critic and helper with this book.

Harvey F. Kline
Hadley, Massachusetts

1

The Land and the People

Colombia can be described quite simply if one is satisfied with a very general approach. The country covers 1,141,748 square kilometers (440,829 square miles), two-thirds again the size of the state of Texas. Somewhat over 28 million Colombians live in the country, and perhaps as many as a million live illegally in Venezuela and the United States; Colombia is the third most populous Latin American country, ranking behind only Brazil and Mexico. Officially about 22 percent of the people are illiterate. The most recent data available indicate that the most common occupations are in agriculture (36 percent in 1973), the industry that contributes the most to gross domestic product (28 percent in 1977). In 1976 there were 848 inhabitants per hospital bed and 1,859 per doctor; life expectancy was 62.2 years.[1] The per capita gross product was US$1,010 in 1979.[2]

In reality the situation is far more complex, and the purpose of this chapter is to demonstrate some of that complexity, to show that there is no "typical Colombian." To that end, I will discuss regional differences, demographic and racial variations, and social stratification.

GEOGRAPHICAL VARIATIONS AND REGIONALISM

The entire territory of Colombia is in the tropic zone, between the extremes of 12° north latitude and 4° south latitude (see Figure 1.1). While this means that length-of-day variations by time of year are only slight, if any, it surely does not mean that all parts of Colombia are alike or that all are hot. Rather, Colombian geography is one of variation according to the altitude of the location. In the Andean mountain region of the country, for example, in a matter of an hour's automobile trip one can travel between a cool climate where potatoes are the major crop and a warm climate in which coffee and bananas are grown. The variations of altitude and mean temperature of the *departamento* capitals are such that one might live in a Colombia with an average temperature

1

2

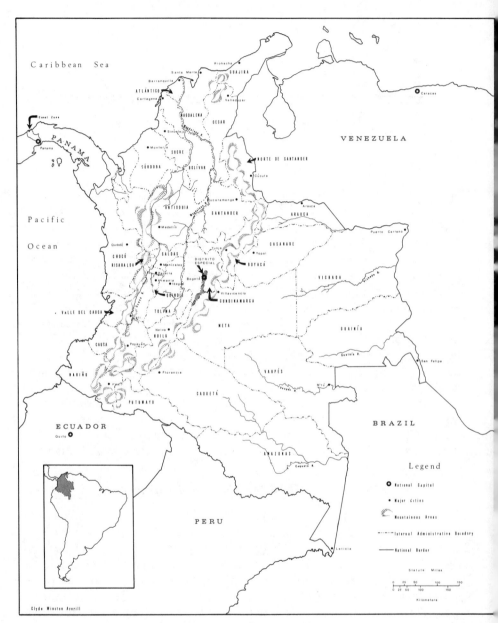

Figure 1.1 Political map of Colombia

of 28° C (82° F) or one of 13° C (55° F)—corresponding to summer in Washington, D.C., and a southern New England spring. One basic reason for these variations is topography. It is difficult to find words that can describe the beauty of the Andes mountains—or describe the obstacles that they cause for the integration of Colombia. The range, which splits into three major cordilleras in the southern part of the country near Ecuador, continues north all the way to the border with Venezuela. The mountains are higher than the Rockies in the United States and, until the advent of air transportation some fifty years ago, made travel between the regions difficult and time-consuming. Even today the trip between the two major cities—Bogotá and Medellín—takes only half an hour by jet, but over a day by bus.

The three ranges of the Andes (called Oriental, Central, and Occidental) are notably different. The Occidental range is the lowest; the highest peak is 4,400 meters (14,436 feet), but most of the other high peaks are between 3,600 and 4,000 meters (11,811 to 13,123 feet). Many of the Occidental mountains are worn by erosion and are thickly vegetated. The Central range is the highest, with a number of permanently snow-covered peaks (despite their being less than 4 degrees from the equator). The highest of these is Sierra Nevada del Huila at 5,429 meters (17,812 feet). The Cordillera Oriental is somewhat lower on average than the Central, although its highest peak (5,493 meters or 18,022 feet) is higher than any in the Central. The Oriental is both the longest and the widest of the three ranges.

Yet the highest peaks in Colombia are not in the Andean mountains, per se, but in the Sierra Nevada of Santa Marta. There the Colón and Bolívar peaks are 5,775 meters (18,947 feet) high and are visible, on a clear day, from the Caribbean beaches of Santa Marta.

With these (and other) topographical variations, it is little wonder that regional differences in Colombia are great. Not only climate varies, but also major economic activities, racial makeup, accent, political behavior, typical foods, religious fervor (although almost all Colombians are at least nominally Roman Catholic, and the nation is, percentagewise, one of the most Catholic in the world), and perhaps even social class relations.

A Colombian can usually identify the regional background of another by his way of speaking, and quite often has a stereotype of the way the individual will act. The stereotype might be that *pastusos* (people from Pasto) are dumb and are the brunt of jokes, as are certain ethnic groups in the United States; that *cachacos* (people from the Bogotá area) are cold, legalistic, and very status conscious; or that *paisas* (people from Antioquia) are religious, hard-working, and have many children. *Costeños* (people from the Caribbean coast) are stereotyped as happy, carefree, capable of drinking large amounts of rum and dancing all night, but not capable of speaking a decent Spanish with final s's pronounced. They do not take the Roman Catholic religion seriously, nor do they take Colombian politics as seriously as their compatriots from the Andean region.[3] Whether or not these stereotypes are empirically valid, they are part of the mythology that makes up the Colombian world view.

Most authorities agree that the three major regions in Colombia are the East, the Andean, and the Caribbean, but there is much disagreement about subregions. For the purpose of this discussion, I follow a recent Colombian typology,[4] which concludes that there are five regions, although three of them are further divided into two subregions each. They are as follows: (1) the Andean East, subdivided into the Cundiboyacense and the Santanderes; (2) the Andean West, subdivided into the West and the Northwest; (3) the Andean South, divided into the Southeast and Tolima Grande; (4) the Caribbean; and (5) the East.

The *departamentos* (departments, administrative divisions roughly comparable to states in the United States) that make up these regions are shown in Table 1.1 (two more have been added since 1973). Characteristics of the capital cities of the *departamentos* are presented in Table 1.2.

The Andean Regions

The most important aspects of Colombia's history have taken place in the Andes mountains. It was in the Andes that the most advanced Amerindians lived; that the Spanish established the major city of the area, Bogotá; that most Colombians have lived (about 75 percent of the people live there today, which is probably the lowest proportion in recent centuries); and that most industry and political activity have been. Until the recent growth of the Caribbean coast, this 30 percent of the territory has been, for all intents and purposes, "Colombia."

Yet the Andes form such formidable barriers that the region has been thought of as having three (or six or even more) subregions. Some parts of the Andes were populated by large numbers of relatively advanced Indians (the Cundiboyacense area) and others by the far reaches of the Inca empire (Nariño). Other areas—intermountain valleys that were warm enough for sugarcane cultivation (Valle del Cauca) and contained gold deposits (Antioquia, Chocó)—had few Indians. Into these areas large numbers of African slaves were imported. Still other areas (such as the Santanderes), where the number of Indians was small, saw the development of small farms and artisan industries. As a result, in the Andean region as a whole—and particularly in the *patrias chicas*

TABLE 1.1
Major Characteristics of Colombian Regions and Departamentos

REGION Subregion Departamento	Percentage of National:		Estimated Population, 1980		
	Terri- tory	Industry	Number (1,000s)	Percentage of national population	Index of growth[a]
ANDEAN EAST	8.6	36.4	9,001	32.9	126
Cundiboyacense	4.1	30.6	6,725	24.6	129
Cundinamarca			5,528	20.2	136
Boyacá			1,197	4.2	105
Santanderes	4.5	5.8	2,276	8.3	118
Santander			1,353	5.0	114
Norte de Santander			923	3.4	126
ANDEAN WEST	12.7	47.9	8,602	31.5	118
West	2.4	nd	3,834	14.0	121
Valle del Cauca			2,965	10.9	126
Risaralda			506	1.9	106
Quindío			363	1.3	108
Northwest	10.3	nd	4,768	17.4	116
Antioquia			3,741	13.4	119
Caldas			760	2.8	103
Chocó			267	1.0	118
ANDEAN SOUTH	9.2	3.2	3,540	13.0	115
Southeast	5.4	1.3	1,921	7.0	118
Nariño			1,073	3.9	120
Cauca			848	3.1	115
Tolima Grande	3.8	1.9	1,619	5.9	112
Tolima			1,052	3.8	110
Huila			567	2.1	114
CARIBBEAN	11.6	12.0	5,412	19.8	125
Atlántico			1,323	4.8	130
Bolívar			1,112	4.1	122
Córdoba			941	3.4	122
Magdalena			710	2.6	114
Cesar			538	2.0	137
Sucre			504	1.8	123
La Guajira			284	1.0	133
EAST	57.8	0.5	771	2.8	101
Meta			361	1.3	140
Others			410	1.5	81
TOTAL	100.0	100.0	27,326	100.0	121

Sources: Atlas Básico de Colombia (Bogotá: Instituto Geográfico "Agustín Codazzi," 1980), passim; Segundo Bernal, "Las regiones colombianas y sus estructuras espaciales," Revista Mensual de Estadística, 346 (Mayo 1980), passim.
[a] 1973 = 100

TABLE 1.2
Characteristics of Major Colombian Cities

REGION Subregion City	Altitude		Mean Temper- ature Degrees:		Estimated Population, 1980		
					Number	Percentage of	
	Meters	Feet	C	F	(1,000s)	Departamento	Nation
ANDEAN EAST							
Cundiboyacense							
Bogotá	2,600	8,530	14	57	4,294	78	16
Tunja	2,820	9,252	13	55	98	8	*
Santanderes							
Bucaramanga	959	3,146	23	73	417	31	2
Cúcuta	320	1,050	26	79	396	43	1
ANDEAN WEST							
West							
Cali	955	3,133	23	73	1,380	46	5
Pereira	1,411	4,629	21	70	262	52	1
Armenia	1,483	4,865	20	68	180	50	1
Northwest							
Medellín	1,479	4,852	20	68	1,574	52	6
Manizales	2,126	6,975	17	62	250	33	1
Quibdó	43	141	28	82	60	22	*
ANDEAN SOUTH							
Southeast							
Pasto	2,527	8,291	14	57	206	19	1
Popayán	1,738	5,702	19	66	115	14	*
Tolima-Grande							
Ibagué	1,285	4,216	21	70	282	27	1
Neiva	442	1,450	26	79	169	30	1
CARIBBEAN							
Barranquilla	68	223	28	82	886	70	3
Cartagena	2	7	28	82	452	34	2
Montería	18	59	28	82	218	23	1
Santa Marta	6	20	27	81	210	28	1
Valledupar	169	554	27	81	277	52	1
Sincelejo	213	699	27	81	110	22	*
Riohacha	3	10	28	82	68	24	*
EAST							
Villavicencio	467	1,532	26	79	145	40	1

Source: Atlas Básico de Colombia (Bogotá: Instituto Geográfico "Agustín
Codazzi," 1980), passim.
*Less than 1 percent.

(feudallike estates run by one or a few families)—an individual was psychologically first a member of the region or the *patria chica* and second a member of the nation.

The *Andean East* has almost one-third of the national population and 36 percent of the national industry in about 8.5 percent of the

Figure 1.2 Andean Colombia: *above*, Laguna La Cocha in Nariño; *below*, coffee growing.

Figure 1.3 Bogotá: the capital and largest city

nation's territory. With the exception of the extremely federal period
of the nineteenth century, described in Chapter 2, the Andean East has
always been the governmental and administrative center of the country.
Besides industry and government, the area is characterized by agriculture
that varies greatly because of the elevation: cultivation of potatoes and
grains in the *sabana* of Bogotá at 2,600 meters (8,530 feet) and Boyacá;
tobacco in the Santanderes; corn, coffee, and citrus fruits at lower
elevations. Indeed, the argument has been made that one reason national
economic integration did not come sooner to Colombia was simply that
all kinds of crops were available near the major cities.

The capital, Bogotá, is in the Andean East. Although Bogotá cannot
compare in size or in percentage of population of the nation with some
of the other metropolises of Latin America, it is growing rapidly now
(50 percent from 1973 to 1980) and is by far the largest Colombian
city, with a full 16 percent of the national population. Its more than
4 million people live in a cool, vernal climate. The original population
was Indian, white, and a mixture of the two (mestizo). Today, because
of in-migration from all parts of the country, *bogotanos* are of all racial
types, and many speak with their regional accents. While the city was
not the original industrial center of Colombia, during the last twenty

Figure 1.4 Medellín

years manufacturing establishments have moved into the area because of the availability of low-priced, abundant labor. Yet most of the employed are in other sectors of the economy, especially that of service.

The *Andean West* constitutes almost 13 percent of the national territory; it has 48 percent of the national industry and 31.5 percent of the population. This very diverse area includes the northwestern *departamento* of Antioquia, with the capital of Medellín, the second-largest city in Colombia and the country's original industrial center. The area also includes the major coffee-producing *departamentos:* Antioquia, Caldas, Quindío, and Risaralda (although coffee is produced in other areas of Colombia also). Further, the western subregion of the Andean West region includes the sugarcane-growing Valle del Cauca, which contains the third-largest Colombian city—Cali.

The economically diverse region is also racially diverse. Valle's population has been strongly influenced by blacks, as has the gold-mining *departamento* of Chocó (which, it should be admitted, is in many ways more like the coastal region than the Andean one). Parts of Antioquia also are heavily influenced by the experience of African

Figure 1.5 Caribbean coastal Colombia: *top,* Tayrona National Park; *bottom,* Santa Marta; *right,* Barranquilla.

slavery; there simply were not enough Indians for the gold-mining activities, and the result is a multiracial society. Whites, blacks, mestizos, mulattos, *zambos,* and perhaps even occasionally one who is racially an Indian can be found in the area.

The Andean West (especially the Antioquia *departamento* and the *departamentos* populated by *antioqueño* migration in the nineteenth century) traditionally has been one of the fastest growing regions, mainly because of large families. As Table 1.1 shows, however, since 1973 the region has been growing more slowly than the nation as a whole.

The *Andean South* is the smallest Andean region in both industry (3.2 percent) and population (13 percent), but not in size (9.2 percent of the national territory, slightly larger than the Andean East). Unlike the other Andean regions and even the coast, it is not characterized by large cities; Ibagué, with a population of 282,000, is the largest. The area is an agricultural one, with variations, as in other Andean regions, according to elevation. Popayán was an important city during colonial times and in the nineteenth century. Today the sleepy city with colonial architecture comes to life only during Holy Week each year, when thousands of Colombian and foreign tourists come to watch the processions, purportedly second only to Seville, Spain, in their splendor.

The Andean South also is diverse racially. The Tolima Grande area is much like the Andean East area, with a combination of individuals of white, Indian, and mestizo racial characteristics. The Southeast subregion, on the other hand, does have large numbers of racial Indians and even some who maintain indigenous dress, artisan products, and language.

The Caribbean Coast

The coastal area of the Caribbean (called the Costa Atlántica by Colombians) makes up almost 12 percent of the national territory. It has about 12 percent of the national industry and 20 percent of the population. In recent years, this has been the area that has grown most rapidly (by 25 percent between 1973 and 1980, for example, when the entire country grew by 21 percent). The climate is hot and harsh, and tropical diseases such as gastroenteritis and malaria are common. Yet recent medical advances (as well as marijuana trade, commerce, and an imminent coal industry) are leading this area to more importance.

The racial characteristics of the Caribbean region are varied, but most notable is the strong influence of black slaves who were brought to this part of Colombia for plantation agriculture, predominantly sugar. Indeed, Cartagena was the major slave port for all of Spanish South America. Barranquilla is a major industrial center, the major port of the country, and its fourth largest city.

The East

The East, almost 60 percent of the national territory, has only 3 percent of the population. The region has two quite distinct subregions. The southern part, which consists of tropical rain forest, is part of the Amazon River basin. Rubber was an important product during the early part of this century; now the region is most important for tourism and the export of animals to zoos of the northern part of the world.

The northern part of the East is part of the Orinoco River basin. Rather than tropical rain forest, it is an area of grasslands, with seasonal floodings. Livestock grazing is the most important economic activity, although some crops are grown (most recently cocaine). It is these Llanos Orientales ("eastern plains") that are the "cowboy" part of Colombia—horses are a common form of transportation; sidearms are not uncommon.

DEMOGRAPHIC CHARACTERISTICS

Racial Relations

One key demographic characteristic—race—was mentioned in the preceding section. One can truly say that Colombians are diverse. There are large numbers of people of pure or nearly pure Spanish background (as well as a smattering of other Europeans, including a small Jewish community whose members arrived mostly at the time of World War II). There are Indians and blacks. There are combinations of the three races, including individuals who are mestizos (white-Indian), mulattos (white-black), and *zambo* (Indian-black). Further, there are people in whose genes are the characteristics of all three races. Having stated this generality of diversity and having pointed out some of the most notable concentrations of various groups, one can go little further. No recent Colombian census has included a question about "race"; anyone who states a figure of the breakdown of the races is but guessing.

There are, however, some things that one can conclude about race in Colombia. First, there is no legal discrimination by race. I have heard rumors of hotels that did not admit blacks, but have never seen evidence of such behavior. However, one's appearance is important, although other forces might be much more so. A friend once told me that when he was growing up in northeastern Cúcuta, it was an advantage for him to have curly hair: in an Indian area, it distinguished him from a racial group characterized by straight hair. Later, when his family moved to Cali (a black-influenced area), his formerly "desirable" curly hair was "undesirable," as clearly it suggested that there might be black background.

Third, many people, especially in the Andean East, who might be racially Indian are not culturally so. In the highlands of Cundinamarca and Boyacá one can see individuals who must be of pure Indian background. However, they are not considered Indian, because they dress in a fashion similar to other inhabitants, and they speak Spanish rather than an indigenous language. Clearly this distinguishes the major part of the Colombian Andes from Ecuador, Peru, and Bolivia.

Fourth, there are *indígenas* (as Colombians called Indians, in both a racial and cultural sense), but they are few. Government statistics indicate that there are 411,803 Indians in the country (or about 1.5 percent of the population). The National Indian Council (Consejo Indígena Nacional) claims to have organized 80 percent of the 700,000 Indians in the country (2.5 percent of the national population); it is of note than it was only in 1982 that the council was founded. Some of these Indians live in the Amazon jungle, in the Guajira Peninsula, and in other isolated rural parts of the country; others live in the Nariño area bordering on Ecuador. Even though there is a newly formed national organization, the Indian question is simply not so salient as in other Andean countries. Indeed, no racial issue is salient politically.

Finally, there is a strong correlation between race and social class. Most—but not all—members of the upper class are of white background. Most—but not all—members of the working classes are people of color.

Figure 1.6 The Colombian East: *above*, the Amazonian rain forest; *below*, the Orinoco Plains.

Figure 1.7 The Colombian people: *above,* Indian workers in the La Guajira salt mines; *below,* middle-class farmers learning about soils.

Figure 1.8 The Colombian people: *left, campesino* children in Boyacá; *below,* picking cotton.

Clearly, other things being equal, it is better to be white than not—but other things are rarely equal. (See the section on "Social Stratification" below.) One can, given the opportunity, move from one "racial" group to another—by moving to the city, by speaking Spanish, by changing dress, by getting an education. Sometimes, however, the opportunity structure through education is not open for people of color—but because of their poverty, not their color.

Population Growth and Urbanization

Colombia in recent years has been a country of both extremely rapid population growth and an increase in the percentage of the people living in urban settings. The country grew from 11.5 million people in 1951 to 17.5 million in 1964, 22.5 million in 1973, and 27.3 million in 1980. These figures indicate growth rates of 3.2 percent per annum between 1951 and 1964; 2.7 percent between 1964 and 1973; and around 2.3 percent since that latter date. At the same time, urban population (defined by the Colombian government as population living in areas of greater than 5,000 people) has increased from 38.9 percent in 1951 to 63.6 percent in 1973. Both sets of data indicate a country dramatically different from that of thirty years ago.[5]

The growth rate, once one of the fastest in the world, has decreased. It is clear that the original increase (after World War II especially) was due to the lower infant mortality that came about with public health programs and greater numbers of physicians. At least two causes are given for the recent decrease in growth rate: a family planning program, sponsored by the government despite the presence of an extremely strong Catholic church, and the effects of urbanization. Rural poor people not only were uneducated in birth control methods, but also saw a certain logic in large families—more children to help in the fields and a form of "social security" for later years. These same people, when living in the cities, needed neither the work force nor the social security of the family. Of course, there was a lag before behavioral patterns changed.

Nevertheless, one should not be hypnotized by the change of growth rate. Although the change is important (and bad or good depending on one's values), the population is still growing very rapidly. While Colombia was doubling its population every 22.5 years before (during the 1951–1964 period), the lower growth rate indicates such doubling now would occur in 31.3 years; 628,000 Colombians are still born each year.

The move to the cities has had several causes, with no reliable data to separate them. People have been forced out of the countryside because of political violence (see Chapter 3) and because of the mechanization of agriculture. Others have been "pulled" to the cities by the hope of a better life—better housing, jobs, schools for their children, the "excitement" of living where things are happening. It is not completely clear that the urban immigrants really do have a better life than before—although they might perceive their own lives to be better or the possibilities for their children to be so, whether or not this is objectively true.

Several things do seem to be clear about urbanization. The urban jobs have not been keeping up with the growth of population. Many Colombians have no jobs and have entered the so-called informal sector in which they live a day-to-day existence as extremely small merchants, restaurateurs, or service-sector operatives. Poverty now is more visible in Colombia. This might be because there are more poor people or simply because these poor people are more apparent in the cities than they were on the countryside. The social relationships common in the countryside (specifically the dependency in a patron-client system) are not always replicated in the cities. This suggests a population that *might* be different politically than it was before.

The Role of Colombian Women

The traditional picture of Latin American women—pampered, sheltered, taking care of the children, serving as the religious leader of the family—clearly is no longer true for all, or even most, Colombian women, if indeed it ever was. Nor is it true that women enjoy equality in social or political terms, although notable women in Colombian history can and should be mentioned.

Increasingly women are in the economically active work force (estimated at 26 percent of the work force in 1973—the most recent data, compared to 19 percent in 1951).[6] This has long been the tradition for peasant women and even those of the urban lower classes, for whom one income is simply not enough. Likewise upper-class women have long participated in economic activities, and it has been noted that upper-class women, because they have the ascribed status of their class, legitimately tell men of lower classes what to do.[7] The dramatic changes seem to be occurring in the middle groups of society and in politics.

The most recent data available indicate that university-level education is increasingly a possibility for middle-class women; 30.5 percent of the public university students in 1970 were women, compared to 21.6 percent in 1966 and 17.6 percent in 1962.[8] As public higher education is especially for the middle sectors, this is probably a valid indication of a change in the roles of women.

Women only received the vote in 1954, not because of a feminist

Figure 1.9 The poor in Bogotá: *tugurios* (*above*) near middle-class parts of town and (*below*) beside luxury upper-class apartment building. (Photographs by author.)

Figure 1.10 Colombian women sorting coffee beans

movement, but as a gift from the one military dictator of this century; they first voted in the 1957 constitutional plebiscite. Most recent data indicate that they vote less often than men, and women seldom hold political office. One study showed that, between 1958 and 1972, only 2.1 percent of the senators, 4.2 percent of the chamber members, 7.4 percent of the members of the departmental assemblies, and 6.4 percent of the municipal councils were women.[9] Yet this clearly is higher than in the period before 1958, when women did not have the right to vote or to hold public office.

Two women—Bertha Hernández de Ospina and María Eugenia Rojas de Moreno—have been the most important ones in Colombian politics in the last decade. Yet the fact that Doña Bertha was the wife of a former president and María Eugenia the daughter of the military dictator indicates important characteristics of women in politics: most are married, and those who either are important leaders (Bertha) or presidential candidates (María Eugenia) have familial relationships with very important men.

It is impossible to remove the role of women from that of their social class. Women can reach the top in politics or in private enterprise, but clearly it is better to be a man, just as in the case of race it is better to be white.

SOCIAL STRATIFICATION AND ECONOMIC INEQUALITY

Economic inequality is a salient characteristic of Colombian society. One does not need statistics to show it; it is enough to see adults picking food out of garbage cans as cars that cost US$50,000 are driven past them or to see shanties of tin and cardboard built beside luxury houses. A few cold numbers, however, can supplement possible non-random impressions.

In 1960, 62.5 percent of all agricultural holdings were less than 5 hectares (12.3 acres). These plots occupied 4.5 percent of all agricultural land. On the other extreme, 0.07 percent of the holdings were greater than 2,500 hectares (6,173 acres), making up 20.2 percent of the land. In 1970–1971, after more than a decade of agrarian reform, even though there were fewer *minifundios* (the very small holdings), there were *more latifundios* of more than 2,500 hectares.[10] In effect, after a decade of land reform there were more superlarge areas occupying more, in absolute terms, of the national territory.

All studies of income distribution conclude that there is a high level of inequality in Colombia. The top decile of the earners and of the households is typically reported to have between 40 and 50 percent of the income, while the bottom quintile (20 percent) has between 2.5 and 5 percent. Income distributions tend to be more inequitable in rural areas than in urban ones.[11] There is disagreement about whether, over the past decade or so, income distribution has become more or less equitable,[12] but it is clear to me that any changes have been slight.

Yet social stratification in Colombia reflects more than inequitable distribution of wealth, however glaring its manifestations. Colombia's class system is based on occupation, education, race, and other factors and, as such, is a more rigid system than most people in the United States are accustomed to seeing.

In broad terms (although there might be regional differences), the great division in Colombia, as in many other places in Latin America, is between a class that does manual labor and one that has occupations that require mental effort. Anecdotal evidence abounds concerning what *gente buena* ("good people," or people in the mental group) should not do: they don't carry their own groceries, wash their own clothes, clean their own houses, repair their own cars, and so on. Other information suggests that people in higher-income levels of the "manual" class might eat better than people of similar incomes in the "mental" class, as the latter have to spend a greater proportion of their income on hired help and on symbols of their prestige—automobiles, clothing, and other consumer goods.

Clearly one's ability to be in the mental class depends on education, and some sons and daughters of the manual class use education to move up to the mental group. Yet often such mobility is not possible. Education (even free public education) for low-income families has a cost in terms of lost employment opportunities. These families need the incomes, meager as they might be, of their children. In addition, public education is insufficient in coverage and sometimes poor in its quality. At the public university level, it is sometimes frustrated by political activities that lead to the closing of the universities.

There is further stratification within the two large classes. Within the mental group, the ideal member of the "oligarchy" (as the Colombians themselves call it) has very high income, is of pure Spanish background and even from one of the traditional families (those that have surnames that indicate *abolengo* or "pedigree"), has received university education abroad or at one of the prestigious private Colombian universities, and belongs to the prestigious private clubs. This oligarchy, some believe, also exercises political power.[13] Probably few people meet all of these requisites, and various combinations no doubt exist.

Within the manual group there is stratification along income lines, with the top groups having well-paid unionized jobs. In the lowest group are the so-called *marginales*, the marginal people who have shanties for dwellings (or none at all) and whose income is from petty commercial activities (selling candy, gum, cigarettes, and the like on the streets), from crime, or (to take the example that most impressed me) from picking through garbage cans or the municipal dump. It is reasonable for members at the top income levels of the manual group to think that mobility, through education, might be possible for their children; it is *not* likewise possible for the very poorest members of the manual class.

Finally, one should not omit the "middle class," at least because it is commonly talked about in Colombia today. No doubt there are increasing numbers of middle-income people with "mental" occupations—doctors, lawyers, and government bureaucrats as well as non-manual employees in private businesses. Their status is ambiguous and their income, with the rapid inflation of recent years, is increasingly tenuous. Their aspirations are not unlike those of their richer colleagues in the mental classes—consumer goods, prestige symbols, good education for their children. They most commonly would send their children to private primary and secondary educational institutions, which are seen to be better than the public ones, and if possible to the most prestigious—

Figure 1.11 Supplementing the family income—buying and reselling newspapers in Bogotá. (Photograph by author.)

and presumably best—ones, so that their children will then have the opportunity to be admitted to the most prestigious private universities. They clearly, especially the wage earners among them, feel the effects of inflation much more than their richer colleagues, who often can hide their real income better. This middle class may have developed (or be about to develop) a common identity as a middle group. Maybe someday they will even form middle-class interest groups and political parties. To this point they have not.

CONCLUSION

From the above it should be obvious that great care must be taken in using the term "Colombia." Clearly there are dramatic differences in the country caused by region, race, sex, income, and social class. While this same statement no doubt also could be made about most countries of the world, one might argue that—because of geography if nothing else—the differences in Colombia are more dramatic than in most countries. Air transport, internal migration, radio and television, and other "modern" phenomena are leading to a more unified nation.

But social class distinctions—as well as those of race and sex—seem to be changing more slowly.

These same differences are seen in Colombian culture. Just as one might argue that there is no one "Colombia," but many, one can also argue that there are various cultures. "Culture" depends on the social class and the region of the country.

Upper- and Middle-class Culture

In the upper- and middle-class Colombian home, albeit with slight regional differences, "culture" is much like that of educated people in Europe or the United States. Music listened to includes the "great masters" of European classical music, although perhaps with more from the Mexican Carlos Chávez or the Brazilian Hector Villalobos. Young people prefer "top twenty" and disco; they frequent night spots that feature such music. Dress is generally along the same lines as in advanced industrial countries. The common alcoholic beverages are Scots whiskey (which also invariably is served at governmental social functions) and imported wines.

The Colombian upper- and middle-class home is characterized by even more electrical paraphernalia than that of the United States— microwave ovens, color television sets, and the ubiquitous "Betamax" (as all video recorders are called), all of which are imported. At Christmastime the gifts bought in local shopping centers are generally imported and include such well-known brands as Wilson sporting goods and Fisher-Price toys. In short, there is little to distinguish culture in those middle- and upper-class Colombian homes from that in the United States and western Europe.

Lower-class Culture

It is in the lower classes that culture varies by region. Since imported whiskey is prohibitively expensive, the common beverages include *aguardiente* (an anise sugarcane liquor) in the Andean parts of the country, *ron blanco* (white rum) in the Caribbean coastal area, and the excellent (and comparatively inexpensive) Colombian beer throughout the country. Music of the "popular" classes includes rapid, rhythmic genres in different parts of the Caribbean coast and slower and more melodious variants in the Andes.

The urban poor often aspire to dress as their middle- and upper- class country people do, although the financial abilities of the poor do not match their aspirations. The rural poor still dress in ways traditional to their regions, although decreasingly so. In Antioquia the *campesino* still arrives in Medellín with his machete over one shoulder and his *carriel* (a type of pocketbook for men, traditionally made of cowhide with the hair still remaining) over the other. In the Caribbean coastal region one can still see the sombrero with intricate patterns made from yellow and black straw. In the higher elevations of the Andes (Cundinamarca and Boyacá, for example) a common outer garment still is the *ruana*, a poncholike covering made from heavy wool. Indeed the *ruana* is so practical, and often so beautiful, that it is commonly used by the middle- and upper-classes.

Gabriel García Márquez

Perhaps all of these divisions of Colombian culture—class and regional—can best be symbolized by one man, the Colombian novelist Gabriel García Márquez. Born in the Caribbean coastal town of Aracataca on March 6, 1928, García Márquez was one of sixteen children of a telegraph operator. In his youth he was sent to a high school in Zipaquirá, a small town near Bogotá. He later had a brief career as a law student and then became a journalist.[14] Colombian regional differences play important roles in his writing. One of the first of his pieces that I read, in the late 1960s, was a Sunday magazine article in which he recounted his impressions when first arriving in the Andean part of the country. The recurring phrase of the article referred to the *cachacos* who wore black and carried black umbrellas. This attire must indeed have been shocking to a young *costeño* used to bright (and less) clothing.

In the 1970s García Márquez was one of the founders of a radical magazine, *Alternativa*. The articles in the magazine, some written by García but more by others, criticized the Colombian establishment, took the side of the poor and organized labor, and, in general terms, called for massive social and economic changes in Colombia. Because of these activities, García Márquez was involved in national politics and was even suggested by some as a possible presidential candidate of the Left. He has, by his own admission, never been a member of a Communist party, although he is a personal friend of Fidel Castro.

In recent years García Márquez most commonly has lived outside of Colombia, mostly in Mexico and Spain. He most recently left his native land in March 1981 when he insisted that he had information that he was about to be arrested under President Turbay's Security Statute (see Chapter 4). Although the government denied such plans, García's reply was that the civilians in the government did not know, or control, what the military was doing.

It was for this reason that Gabriel García Márquez was in Mexico City when, in October 1982, he was awarded the 1982 Nobel Prize for Literature. Comparing him to Balzac and Faulkner, the selection committee stated that "Each new work of his is received by expectant critics and readers and as an event of world importance, is translated into many languages and published as quickly as possible in large editions."[15] This prize was recognition of García Márquez's position as a leading novelist worldwide and of his being one of the leaders of the "boom" of Latin American literature that began in the 1960s. While the Nobel Prize is not for a specific work, his most notable has been *Cien Años de Soledad* (*One Hundred Years of Solitude*), a chronicle of the mythical Buendía family of the mythical town of Macondo.

García Márquez has always been somewhat ambivalent about recognition. To friends anticipating his receiving the 1982 Nobel Prize, he said that it would be "good for the revolution" in Latin America, but he also has commented that "the worst thing that can happen to a writer in a continent where people don't read is that his books are sold like sausages."[16] His ambivalence might be based on the fact that, within Colombia, the individuals who have enough education to read his books are *not* the ones who are likely to agree with his politics. The lower classes, who allegorically are the heroes of his novels, many times cannot read them.

NOTES

1. *Atlas Básico de Colombia* (Bogotá: Instituto Geográfico "Agustín Codazzi," 1980), p. 6.

2. World Bank, *World Development Report 1981* (Washington, D.C.: World Bank, 1981), p. 134.

3. These regional differences are seen well in the works of world-famous Colombian novelist Gabriel García Márquez, himself a *costeño*.

4. Segundo Bernal, "Las regiones colombianas y sus estructuras espaciales (resumen)," *Revista Mensual de Estadística* 346 (1980): 7–62.

5. *Atlas Básico de Colombia* (Bogotá: Instituto Geográfico "Agustín Codazzi," 1980), p. 6.

6. Cecilia López de Rodríguez and Magdalena León de Leal, "El Trabajo de la Mujer," in Magdalena León de Leal, ed., *La Mujer y el Desarrollo en Colombia* (Bogotá: ACEP, 1977), p. 195.

7. Steffen W. Schmidt, "Women in Colombia: Attitudes and Future Perspectives in the Political System," *Journal of Interamerican Studies and World Affairs* 17, no. 4 (1975): 469.

8. Ibid., p. 469.

9. Shirley Harkness and Patricia Pinzón de Lewin, "Women, the Vote, and the Party in the Politics of the Colombian National Front," *Journal of Interamerican Studies and World Affairs* 17, no. 4 (1975): 443.

10. Calculated from data presented in Julio Silva Colmenares, *Los Verdaderos Dueños del País* (Bogotá: Fondo Editorial Suramérica, 1977), p. 233.

11. Albert Berry and Ronald Soligo, "The Distribution of Income in Colombia: An Overview," in R. Albert Berry and Ronald Soligo, eds., *Economic*

Policy and Income Distribution in Colombia (Boulder, Colo.: Westview Press, 1980), p. 5.

12. Miguel Urrutia, as he stated on Bogotá television in 1981, believes that income distribution is now more equitable than it was ten years ago. R. Albert Berry believes that it is more inequitable (conversation with the author, Washington, D.C., November 1981).

13. Colombian social scientists (especially those from the Left) constantly refer to *la oligarquía*. For a North American's attempt to show empirically that it does not exist, see James J. Payne, "The Oligarchy Muddle," *World Politics* 20 (1968): 439–453.

14. Marlise Simons, "Storyteller with Bent for Revolution: Gabriel García Márquez," *New York Times* October 22, 1982, A10.

15. Quoted in John Vinocur, "García Márquez Wins Nobel; Radical Colombian Novelist," *New York Times* October 22, 1982, A1.

16. Quoted in Simons.

2

Colombian History: From Indian Times to 1930

The past always plays a part in contemporary events. This chapter sketches the history before 1930 of the area we now call Colombia. My major interest is to present themes that became "historical givens" by the end of the period.

HISTORY TO 1830

Amerindian Communities and Spanish Colonization

At least eight different Amerindian linguistic groups lived in Colombia at the beginning of the sixteenth century, perhaps totaling as many as 700,000 people. Some were warlike hunters and fishers, including the Caribs and Arawaks. Many had developed agriculture, as well as gold work (now beautifully collected in the Museo de Oro in Bogotá) that attracted the Spanish conquerors. But by far the most "advanced" Indian group was the Chibchas (more properly Muiscas) who populated the highland areas of today's *departamentos* of Cundinamarca and Boyacá. The Chibchas had the most wealth, had established densely settled agricultural communities, and had developed a relatively advanced sociopolitical organization headed by three leaders called the Zipa, the Zaque, and the Iraca.[1]

Later exploration demonstrated that some advanced Indian groups, for unknown reasons, had disappeared by the time the Spanish arrived. The most notable of these was the civilization in the valley of San Agustín, in the south of the *departamento* of Huila. While the Indians were no longer there, the signs of their culture were, including temples and large statues.

The first Spaniard to reach the shores of Colombia was Alfonso de Ojeda, who explored the Guajira coast in 1500. In 1509 the same

29

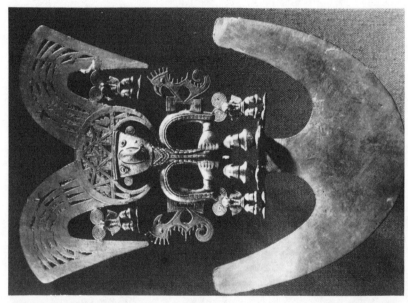

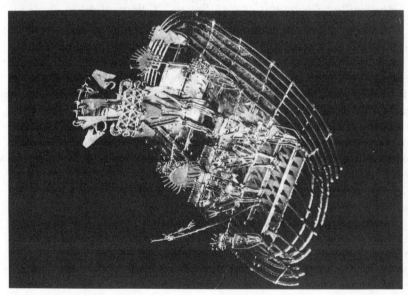

Figure 2.1 Amerindian gold work: *left*, golden raft depicting a chief surrounded by priests and slaves enroute to a ritual bath; *right*, a gold breast piece.

Figure 2.2 Statues in San Agustín, Department of Huila

Ojeda was the first to found a settlement near Cartagena, although it did not last. The first permanent settlements were in Cartagena (1533) and Santa Marta (1535).

The city of Santa Fe de Bogotá was founded in 1538 by Gonzalo Jiménez de Quesada. In an irony of history, two other conquerors independently reached the city the following year: Sebastián de Belalcázar, from Ecuador; and Nikolaus Federmann, from Venezuela. In 1549 an *audiencia* was established in the city and in 1563 a capitancy general.

The first 200 years were ones of ineffectual government and regionalism—themes that continue until this century. The capitancy general was formally part of the viceroyalty of Peru, centered in the far-off city of Lima. Distance made it difficult for the viceroy to maintain effective control on the *capitán general* in Bogotá. Further, within the capitancy general, the leader in Bogotá had great difficulty in maintaining his own effective control over the leaders in the six parts of the capitancy general: Cartagena, Santa Marta, Riohacha, Antioquia, Popayán, and Panamá. Indeed it might be argued that the Catholic church was a more efficacious organization than the government was. The archbishop in Bogotá, as well as bishops in the six mentioned regions, and five major Catholic orders (Franciscan, Augustinian, Jesuit, Capuchin, and Dominican) no doubt had better organizations than the Spanish empire did.[2]

The capitancy general was not a backwater of Spanish colonization, nor was it a principal center like Lima or Mexico. Cartagena developed into a major port through which all trade with South America was supposed to flow (including the silver of Peru). A small number of Spanish colonizers came for Colombia's natural riches, especially gold and emeralds. The *encomienda* (a system through which the Spanish Crown granted Indians to landowners, who were to care for and Christianize the Indians in return for their work) existed in some parts of the area, but the lack of relatively advanced and peaceful Indians limited this institution to highland regions, especially the Chibcha area. African slaves were brought into sometimes rich sugar areas of the Caribbean coast. Miscegenation began throughout the capitancy general.

In 1739 Bogotá became the capital of the new viceroyalty of Nueva Granada (including today's countries of Colombia, Panama, Venezuela, and Ecuador). The area then had relatively more importance for the few years before the independence movement.

The Wars of Independence and Gran Colombia

It is noteworthy that one of the cities of Colombia (Cartagena in May 1810) declared its own independence before anyone made such a statement for the entire viceroyalty. After Bogotá declared independence

Figure 2.3 The San Felipe de Barraja fortress, Cartagena

(July 20, 1810), the following six years were called by later Colombians "The Foolish Fatherland" (*Patria Boba*), although there was more "foolishness" than "fatherland" in the new South American country. Parts of the country never declared independence (Popayán, Panamá, Santa Marta), and those parts that did proved unable to cooperate with each other. Given these circumstances it was not surprising that the Spanish were able to reconquer the territory in 1815–1816.

Definitive independence for Colombia came in August 1819 with the militarily unimportant battle of Boyacá. The Spanish were defeated in this battle by patriot forces led by the Venezuelan Simón Bolívar after a lightning trip up the mountains from the Orinoco region. So Colombian independence came the second time around, and the new leader was a Venezuelan who already recognized that there were regional differences.

In 1821, through the Constitution of Cúcuta, a government was set up for the entire old viceroyalty, which was called Gran Colombia. Bolívar continued south to fight for the independence of Ecuador (1822) and Peru and Bolivia (1824), leaving behind his vice president, the Colombian Francisco de Paula Santander, to govern the new nation.

Yet—given already existing regional identities and problems of transportation—the new country was doomed from the start. In 1827 Bolívar returned to Bogotá, finding that unity was breaking down. He tried to force a strong government, near to a constitutional monarchy, only to discover resistance to Venezuelans, military people, and strong government. Bolívar managed to establish a dictatorship without constitutional sanction in 1828 and he survived an assassination attempt, but Gran Colombia was breaking up. Bolívar resigned in March 1830 and died in December of the same year.

The failure of Gran Colombia showed an important theme that continued in the following years: the elite in Colombia had already developed a civilian mystique, a characteristic that restricted military dictatorships to only one in the nineteenth century and one in the twentieth, distinguishing the country from most others in Latin America. Three arguments have been used to explain this anomaly. First, the military establishment that brought independence was not Colombian, but rather mostly Venezuelan. Second, the civilian elite in Colombia, unlike that in other countries, was not destroyed by the independence wars. And finally, the military men who brought independence were not only Venezuelan, but were men of color (not Bolívar, but surely many of his officers), a condition not acceptable to the white *gente buena* of Bogotá.[3] Whatever the reasons (no doubt a combination of some of the above, plus others), the mystique of "democracy" developed from this point.

THE FIRST CENTURY OF
COLOMBIAN INDEPENDENCE, 1830–1930

After the failure of the Gran Colombia experiment, the country we now call Colombia was on its own as an independent country (although until 1863 called Nueva Granada). After a few years of personalist struggle, factions became organized, and the political parties that have so dominated national life were formed.

The Pre-1849 Period and
the Formation of Political Cleavages

Politics in the early years of the country were personalistic and volatile, just what one would expect when the legitimate authority of the Crown (and Bolívar, a foreigner but the liberator) had been removed. The writing of the constitution continued, with more concern for contemporary European ideologies than national reality. Regionalism continued to be important: the viceroyalty had never integrated the country, and the independence wars had not either. There were new conflicts between leaders who had participated in the wars of independence and those who had not. The country was poor and only slightly inhabited (the first census in 1851 showed a population of only 2.25 million). Most people lived in quasi-feudal situations, as the clients of large landowners (*patrones*), and the cities were very small. The state was weak. Although there were some economic benefits for groups who obtained control of the state, the bureaucratic positions and tax collections were not sufficient to satisfy those controlling groups.[4]

The first civil war (of eight in the nineteenth century) took place between 1838 and 1842. The war began with what appeared to be a trivial event: the abolishment of small monasteries in Nariño. But this occurred in a society that included deep-rooted religious values, religious groups that had had great difficulty in surviving, and a church that was already powerful. Landowners also were searching for an excuse for a conflict, albeit over different issues. For these reasons the conflict lasted long and spread throughout the country.

The personalist nature of politics began abating with the government in power from 1845 to 1849: political representatives of the merchants started to play a larger role in government, at the invitation of the government itself. By 1849 there was an alternative form of social organization to that of the colonial latifundia: mercantile capital. While the changes were hesitant at first, they laid the ground for those that were to occur after 1850. As the governments, to this point, had been protectionist in their tariff policies, artisan development had been encouraged. By 1846 numerous urban groups had formed, promoted by merchants connected with the artisans and by a group of young lawyers. These artisan groups came to be called "democratic societies"; their membership was not limited to artisans, and they grew rapidly. In competition with this type of political organization, the Jesuits founded "popular" or "Catholic" societies after 1849, which were never very successful. By 1850 the major cities had many of both societies.

The social basis was thus laid for the creation of political parties in 1849. On one side were the traditional *latifundistas*, in alliance with the Catholic church; on the other, the merchants and the artisans.

These differences became more crystalized during the government of General Jose Hilario López (1849–1853), who was elected by the National Congress under considerable pressure from the artisan groups. The López government was one in which the political representatives of the merchants were able to implement a series of reforms that destroyed the colonial institutional structure. As Francisco Leal has argued, "In essence, these reforms sought to create economic bases which would substitute for, or at least liberate the merchants from the political class domination of large landowners whose power base lay in the 'static' social organization inherited from the colonial period."[5] The major reforms included abolition of the tobacco monopoly, which meant free cultivation and commercialization of the crop; a suspension of the institution of the *censos* (church mortgages) when the state in 1851–1852 took them over; the elimination of Indian reservations in 1850, making possible the commercialization of their land and the freeing of Indian labor; a direct form of taxation (1850–1851), based on a fiscal and administrative decentralization; and emancipation, in 1851, of the 20,000 remaining slaves. It is not surprising that a civil war broke out in 1851 in the west and central regions of the country— regions in which the latifundia organization was based predominantly on slavery.

Political Parties and Patterns of Behavior for the New Nation

The two parties—Liberal and Conservative—that continue until today were established in 1849, and by the end of the López government had become somewhat organized. Their first programs appeared at their founding, although it must be admitted that the programs showed great similarity. Both defended liberty, justice, order, and political and religious tolerance. Both were averse to dictatorships and stated that they were democratic.[6]

Over the years that followed, certain patterns of political behavior developed, which still affect Colombian political behavior today.

Ideological Differences. The two parties soon developed different programs that were, at least to a certain degree, carried out when the respective parties came to power.[7] The Liberals were for federalism and free trade and were anticlerical. The Conservatives favored unitary government and protectionism and were proclerical. There were notable exceptions to these generalizations, including a Conservative president who was instrumental in the approval of a federalist constitution.

In essence, the ideological difference came to be one about the proper role of the Roman Catholic church in the society. While the Liberals were surely Catholic (and at times made specific efforts to demonstrate that they were not antichurch), they opposed an active clergy outside of the religious sphere. Indeed, part of the intensity involved in the political struggles of the nineteenth century was because of the religious aspect of the struggle. It has been argued that the Conservatives used their proclerical position to mobilize the masses: "There remained only one road that opened the access to the masses [for the Conservative party]. . . . The only Conservative banner which had life and demonstrated resolution and vigor was that which used religious sentiments. *Rojismo* [Liberalism] had no other enemy in New Granada which could confront it except Catholicism."[8]

A declaration of Holy War was extremely clear as early as 1853 when an *Exposición Católica*, written by the Conservative Rufino Cuervo, was read in all the churches of Bogotá and later disseminated throughout the country. The Conservative party was the beneficiary of this exposition.

The religious aspect of the party conflict soon added intensity to the partisan conflict. While Colombians could agree to disagree about the other parts of the party programs, they could not easily accept disagreement about the religious question. As the Colombian sociologist Fals Borda has argued,

> This religious struggle—emotional, bitter, and personal—made the consciousness of social class pass to a second level and eliminated the conflicts based on popular self-identification. The Colombian political parties were converted to simple agglomerations in which there remained together both members of the elite and of the lower classes who had their inclinations. . . . For this reason, far from being an "element of national unity" and of "social order," as the Constitution says, the Catholic religion has really been a source of conflict and a root of the bitter disunion between Colombians.[9]

This religious aspect of the conflict increased after 1861, when a Liberal government confiscated church lands. It is estimated that the Catholic church owned one-third of the land at the time.

Multiclass Parties. Colombian parties have always been multiclass ones. This means that both parties have always had both elite and mass sectors; it also means that the elite divisions have never been neat. While it may be argued that the original elite division was between the colonial latifundia group (the Conservatives) and the mercantile-capital one (the Liberals), the two groups also realized that they had interests in common. The colonial *latifundistas* soon understood the direction of change and hurried to adapt themselves to it and to get everything possible from new conditions, even federalism and free trade. Both groups realized that they could put their differences aside when power seemed to be increasing for members of the middle or popular classes, as in the 1854 coup of General Melo (the only military government of the century).[10] While many things divided the Conservatives and Liberals, both were from the elite of the society and hence many things united them. Indeed, the dividing line between the two groups was never completely clear: merchants might be latifundia owners who were temporarily converted into speculators and usurers; merchants dependent on the incipient foreign trade, whose clients were the latifundia owners; or merchants supported by the limited agricultural and artisan commercialization.[11]

Violent Conflict. Political competition was not limited to peaceful means; there were eight civil wars during the nineteenth century, six of which pitted all (or part) of one party against the other party. As a result of these civil wars (which, in total, lasted eleven of the sixty-three years between 1839 and 1902), the peasant masses "participated" in national politics and knew of the national political system. Of course this did not mean that the masses had influence on the policies of the elites. Most of the mass participation was originally because of their adscription to a *patrón*, who instructed them to fight.

The longest, cruelest, and most devastating of these violent conflicts between the two parties was the War of the Thousand Days, which began in July 1899 with a Liberal revolt aimed to unseat the Conservative government. Beginning in the *departamento* of Santander, the conflict soon spread to other *departamentos*. The largest battle was that of Palonegro (near Bucaramanga, Santander) in May 1900, in which 15,000 government troops defeated 14,000 Liberal rebels. After the first nine months of the war, as Colombian historians later recalled, "The soil of the fatherland was inundated with blood, thousands of Colombians died on the battle fields, there was a considerable number of wounded in the hospitals, and the country found itself completely ruined."[12] Yet the war continued until June 1902 (and did, quite literally, last about a thousand days). At the end of the conflict, the balance sheet included more than 100,000 men dead, more with disabling injuries, commerce ruined, difficult communications, economic production almost nil, and a paper currency (used by the government to finance the war) that had a paper peso that was worth less than a gold centavo.[13] A bit over a year later, as described in the next section, another cost of the loss of the war was, in part, the *departamento* of Panamá.

Intense Party Identification. The numerous civil wars and the widespread participation of the *campesinos* ("peasants") in them led to a strict and intense partisan socialization of the masses. Many (if not most) *campesino* families had "martyrs," family members who had been killed, disabled, or raped by members of the other political party. While original party identification of *campesinos* came from those of their *patrones*, at some point this identification developed a life of its own, based on the past. As Eduardo Santa, a Colombian sociologist, has argued, Colombians began to be born "with party identifications attached to their umbilical cords."[14] As a result, other cleavages (such as social class and regionalism) became secondary to the primary party one. Third parties were (and are) notably unsuccessful.

Party Government. The mystique of civilian, "democratic" government begun earlier continued. "Democratic" government meant party government. In the nineteenth century there were only three dictatorships (only one of which was a military one). None lasted more than one and a half years and all were terminated by partisan opposition.

Coalitions. While the masses learned to hate each other and died for their parties, elite party members quite often entered into bipartisan electoral and governmental coalitions (see Table 2.1), a tendency that continues to this century. These coalitions tended to occur when there were arbitrary executives, when party hegemonies shifted, and, particularly in the current century, when the elite-instigated violence got out of hand.[15] Indeed, it might be argued that the elites have not taken the party identification so seriously as the masses have, for if they had, they could not have agreed to so many coalitions.

Federalism to Centralism. The country experimented with both extreme federalism and centralism during the nineteenth century. Through the constitutions of 1853, 1858, and 1863, Colombia became one of the most federalist systems of the world; indeed, perhaps a better term would be "confederal." According to the Rionegro Constitution (1863), the federated states had sovereignty, with the central government having only the powers of foreign relations and some powers in the case of foreign wars. There were no limits to individual liberties; each state had its own army. It has been reported that Victor Hugo (considered by the Colombians to be the intellectual author of the Rionegro Constitution) remarked, when Colombians delivered him a copy, "This must be a country of angels."[16]

There was, under the Rionegro Constitution, complete freedom in arms production and traffic. Civil wars and violence throve. Between 1863 and 1885 there were more than fifty insurrections, as well as forty-two different constitutions in the nine states.[17]

This extreme federalism continued until 1885, when the Conservatives and the Independent Liberals formed a coalition, known as the "National party," to support Rafael Núñez in what was to be called the Regeneration. While the National party did not last long, the Constitution of 1886 (albeit greatly amended) remains in force until this day. This constitution reversed the earlier federal trend and brought the República de Colombia into a strongly centralist mode. No longer would the national government in Bogotá be weak. No longer would the president of Colombia be a lesser *caudillo* than those who ran the federal states under the Rionegro Constitution. Rather, the president

TABLE 2.1
Bipartisan Coalitions in Colombian History, 1854-1949

Years	Name	Participants	Purpose and Stipulations
1854	---	Conservatives	Against dictatorship of Melo; two secretaries of state, one from each party.
1854	---	Conservatives Radical Liberals	To elect Mallarino vice president
1857	National Party	Parts of both parties	To support candidacy of Mosquera
1867	---	Conservatives Radical Liberals	Against strong government of Mosquera
1869	---	Conservatives Radical Liberals	To elect Mosquera; equal representation in Congress and other public corporations; mutual assent on all political problems.
1883-1886	National Party	Conservatives, Independent Liberals	In support of Núñez and his "regeneration." Began as an attempt to get all factions into the cabinet, which failed. An attempt to do away with old parties, which failed.
1904-1909	---	Parts of both parties	As part of reconciliation after War of the Thousand Days; two Liberals in cabinet of six.
1909-1914	Republican Union	Parts of both parties	Against strong government of Reyes; after his fall, continued through sharing of cabinet posts.

would name the governors of the *departamentos.* No longer would there be state militias.

Elite Factions. The elites of the two parties tended to split into factions. It was (and is) quite common for the elite of any party to be divided on ideology, sector of the economic elite, personalism, and perhaps even regionalism. (Quite often these criteria were not mutually exclusive.) The masses, on the other hand, tended to be either Liberals or Conservatives simply (*a secas*). If masses shifted from one faction of their party to another, it was because their leaders (*patrones, gamales*— rural leaders who behaved in patronage networks, or other "natural leaders") shifted in clique affiliation. Neither masses nor their leaders, however, shifted from one party to the other.

TABLE 2.1 (cont.)
Bipartisan Coalitions in Colombian History, 1854-1949

Years	Name	Participants	Purpose and Stipulations
1914-1922	---	Parts of both parties	A continuation of the Republican Union, without using name. Minority representation of Liberals in the cabinet; support of Moderate Conservative presidential candidate through 1918.
1930-1932	National Concentration	Parts of both parties	In support of Olaya candidacy; Bi-partisan cabinet.
1946	National Union-- Lleras C.	Liberals, Moderate Conservatives	Political conflict over López; general instability; three Moderate Conservatives in cabinet
1946-1948; 1948-1949	National Union-- Ospina	Liberals, Moderate Conservatives	In support of candidacy of Ospina; after election, in response to being a minority president and to the violence, especially after the death of Gaitán. Cabinet divided equally, with six from each party; "crossover" system in departamentos, with governors and secretaries of government from different parties.

Source: Harvey F. Kline, "The National Front: Historical Perspective and Overview," in R. Albert Berry, Ronald G. Hellman, and Mauricio Solaún, editors, Politics of Compromise: Coalition Government in Colombia (New Brunswick, N.J.: Transaction Books, 1980), pp. 68-69. Reprinted with the permission of the publisher.

These factions of political parties tended to be more predominant when there was no common enemy from the other political party. However, if there was a challenge from the other party (or, at times, from nonelite groups), factional differences could be, and were, put aside.

Coffee, Foreign Investment, Imperialism, and the "Dance of the Millions"

During most of the nineteenth century, Colombia was not part, in any meaningful sense, of the "international system." Economically the country had no product that could be exported consistently in order to earn foreign exchange. While gold remained important, other crops—

tobacco and quinine, for example—fluctuated greatly. It was only after the 1870s that coffee became an important export, a condition that continues still. With coffee came a new group within the Colombian elite: the coffee merchants. These merchants bought from the growers and sold to foreign roasters. With their surpluses, the merchants entered into other investments, including import substitution industrialization (ISI), especially in Medellín, as early as the first decade of this century.

The first important action of foreign capital during the nineteenth century was giving loans, beginning in the 1820s. Later foreign interests entered into gold production. In the 1880s railroads to the sea or to the Magdalena River became the principal form of foreign investment.

Colombia abruptly entered into the international system in 1903. After the Colombian senate refused to ratify a treaty with the United States for the construction of a canal in the *departamento* of Panamá, the U.S. government of Theodore Roosevelt encouraged a rebellion and prevented Colombian troops from traveling from Cartagena to Colón. The United States quickly recognized the new Republic of Panama and signed a treaty that was even more favorable to the U.S. government than the one not accepted by the Colombian senate.[18]

In the years that followed the rape of Panama, Colombia entered more than previously into a system of economic dependence on the United States. This process had begun already with coffee cultivation. While foreign interests have never owned the lands on which the coffee is grown, most coffee that is exported is sold to U.S. roasters. In the first decade of this century, the United Fruit Company (UFCO) arrived in the Caribbean coastal regions, buying land and setting up "banana enclaves." By the 1920s, Colombian army troops were assisting UFCO by putting down labor-union activities.

The period of dependency became most apparent during the 1920s in a "Dance of the Millions." US$173 million were borrowed by the Colombian government in this decade. Another US$25 million came when the government of the United States paid an "indemnity" for the loss of Panama. In the latter case, it has been argued by both North American and Colombian scholars that the message was delivered—in a tacit if not explicit form—that the indemnity would be paid if, and only if, U.S. petroleum companies were allowed to enter the country. Standard Oil of New Jersey was allowed in, even before the indemnification was made.[19] Gulf came a few years later. Both were awarded long-term concessions.

By the late 1920s, Colombia had become a much more complex country. Foreign interests were important for the first time. New economic groups had arisen with import substitution industrialization and with creation of a larger financial sector. Some mass groups, including both unionized workers and the rural *campesinos* who had little or no land, were becoming restless with the status quo. With the crisis of the Great Depression—as well as divisions within the ruling Conservative party— the Liberals came back to power for the first time since 1885.

CONCLUSION

By 1930 Colombia was no longer a "new nation." The *tabula rasa* (which was never completely *rasa*) that came with the dissolution of Gran Colombia had been filled in. The letter on that tablet (which represented both constraints and advantages for different groups) had been completed, although, of course, parts could have been erased and changed in later years.

Clearly the most important contribution that came from the first 100 years was the creation of a two-party system. The story of Colombia since 1930 is the conflict over which parts of the tradition should be maintained and which parts eliminated.

NOTES

1. *Atlas Básico de Colombia* (Bogotá: Instituto Geográfico "Agustín Codazzi," 1980), p. 15.

2. John Edwin Fagg, *Latin America: A General History* (New York: Macmillan, 1963), p. 361.

3. J. Mark Ruhl, "Civil-Military Relations in Colombia: A Societal Explanation," *Journal of Interamerican Studies and World Affairs* 23, no. 2 (1981): 133.

4. The rest of this section is based on Francisco Leal Buitrago, "Social Classes, International Trade and Foreign Capital in Colombia: An Attempt at Historical Interpretation of the Formation of the State, 1819–1935," Ph.D. dissertation, University of Wisconsin, 1974, pp. 65–81.

5. Ibid., p. 81.

6. Eduardo Santa, *Sociología Política de Colombia* (Bogotá: Ediciones Tercer Mundo, 1964), pp. 44–48.

7. Two North American authors who have argued that ideology has never been very important in Colombian politics are Vernon Lee Fluharty, *Dance of the Millions: Military Rule and the Social Revolution in Colombia 1930–1956*, 2nd ed. (Pittsburgh: University of Pittsburgh Press, 1966); and James L. Payne, *Patterns of Conflict in Colombia* (New Haven: Yale University Press, 1968).

8. Germán Colmenares, *Partidos Políticos y Clases Sociales* (Bogotá: Ediciones Universidad de los Andes, 1968), p. 100.

9. Orlando Fals Borda, *Subversión y Cambio Social* (Bogotá: Ediciones Tercer Mundo, 1968), pp. 101–102.

10. Leal, pp. 88–89.

11. Leal, p. 100.

12. Jesús María Henao and Gerardo Arrubla, *Historia de Colombia*, 8th ed. (Bogotá: Talleres Editoriales de la Librería Voluntad, 1967), p. 814.

13. Ibid., p. 815.

14. Santa, p. 37.

15. These coalitions are discussed in Harvey F. Kline, "The National Front: Historical Perspective and Overview," in R. Albert Berry, Ronald G. Hellman, and Mauricio Solaún, eds., *Politics of Compromise: Coalition Government in Colombia* (New Brunswick, N.J.: Transaction Books, 1980), pp. 59–83.

16. Jaime Jaramillo Uribe, "Etapas y Sentido de la Historia de Colombia," in Mario Arrubia et al., *Colombia Hoy* (Bogotá: Siglo Veintiuno Editores, 1980), p. 46.

17. Leal, p. 112.

18. See Chapter 6 for a more detailed discussion. These events are summarized, among other places, in Federico Gil, *Latin American–United States Relations* (New York: Harcourt Brace Jovanovich, 1971), pp. 126–133.

19. Leal, p. 228; J. Fred Rippy, *The Capitalists and Colombia* (New York: Vanguard Press, 1931), pp. 103–122.

3

Crisis and Conflict: 1930 to the Present

The period since 1930 in Colombian politics has been one of great variations. There have been civil wars (including the most violent and longest of Colombian history), a military dictatorship, and periods of civilian coalition government. Throughout these years the key actors have been the elite sectors of the two political parties, although each party most commonly has been divided into various factions. In this chapter, I hope to give an overview of this varied picture.

CONFLICT AND VIOLENCE, 1930–1958

The period started with a change of party hegemony. In 1930 the Conservatives offered two presidential candidates. The Liberals (together with a group of Moderate Conservatives) offered the candidacy of the then ambassador to Washington, Enrique Olaya Herrera. As had happened in the past (and would happen again in the future), the party of the presidency changed when the dominant party could not agree on a single candidate.

Under the stipulations of the Constitution of 1886, a change of party in the presidency inevitably led to a change in law enforcement policy because the president appointed all the governors (who in turn named all the mayors of the municipalities in their *departamentos*) and all cabinet and subcabinet officials. In the highly partisan Colombian political world, Conservative police officers (appointed by Conservative mayors or governors) were more likely to apply the strict letter of the law to Liberals; likewise, Liberals applied the law more strictly to Conservatives. In these conditions, the election of Olaya led to some violence between the two traditional parties, as well as to violent clashes between police and peasants who attempted to improve their land-tenure situations. This was but an omen of things to come.

45

The Liberal Hegemony, 1930–1946

Factionalism within the two parties, discussed in the preceding chapter, has always been common in Colombia. Nothing happened after 1930 to change that generalization; however, the ideologies and social bases of the factions changed.

In general, the disputes of the previous century about federalism-centralism and the role of the Catholic church had been settled, or at least placed aside, by 1930. The new element was the dispute over the role of the state in the economy. Part of the Liberal party had become supporters of government intervention in the economy and of controlled social change. This change of party program was first suggested by Rafael Uribe Uribe at the beginning of the century, but was not adopted by a party convention until 1922.[1]

Yet the Liberals were not united in this ideology, and the Conservatives, although almost all were against such a role for the state, differed in their oppositions. One can construct a rough right-left continuum on state interventionism that applies not only to the 1930s, but also to the years since in many ways. At the left were the Radical Liberals, favoring social change (albeit controlled); on the right were the "Historical" Conservatives, quite often evoking a corporate–organic state paradigm and calling for the glories of Ferdinand and Isabella of sixteenth-century Spain; in the middle were the "Moderate" Liberals and the "Moderate" Conservatives. These moderate groups favored the status quo and wished for neither a larger role for the state in the economy nor an organic state. These divisions (summarized in Table 3.1) continue to be present.

Yet one should not suggest that ideology was the only factor in factionalism. In part, the factional conflicts were among leaders with forceful personalities, which led to personal animosities. In part, there was a patronage factor. Because all government jobs were part of a spoils system (it was reported that all government jobs changed with the change of party—or faction—all the way down to the maids and doorkeepers in the governmental offices), conflicts occurred over whose followers would get these scarce jobs. Colombian politics continued to center around *roscas*, the personal cliques that included not only highly educated people who might fill ministerial posts but also people of lower social groups who could occupy all kinds of other positions.

Lastly, it has been argued that there was a difference in the sector of the "dominant class" that these factions represented. The Radical Liberals represented the new financial-capital groups; the Historical Conservatives, the traditional latifundia; and the moderate groups, those other, more ambiguous groups, such as export-oriented latifundia and

TABLE 3.1

Party Faction Presidents and Leaders, 1930-1982

Period	Radical Liberals	Moderate Liberals	Moderate Conservatives	Historical Conservatives
1930-46	P: López P., 1934-38, 1942-45.	P: Olaya, 1930-34; Santos, 1938-42; Lleras C., 1945-46.	L: M. Ospina	L: L. Gómez
1946-53	L: Gaitán	L: G. Turbay	P: M. Ospina, 1946-50.	P: L. Gómez, 1950-53.
1953-58 (military government)	L: Lleras R.	L: Lleras C.	L: M. Ospina	L: L. Gómez
1958-74	P: Lleras R., 1966-70. L: López M.	P: Lleras C., 1958-62.	P: Valencia, 1962-66; Pastrana, 1970-74.	L: L. Gómez A. Gómez
1974-82	L: Lleras R. Galán	P: López M., 1974-78; J. Turbay, 1978-82.	L: Pastrana; B. Ospina	P: Betancur, 1982-86 L: A. Gómez

P indicates presidents elected.   L indicates chief leaders.

groups that had interests in several economic activities.[2] The role of the "popular" classes was hence secondary.

While the government of Olaya was a status quo one, he was followed in 1934 by Alfonso López Pumarejo, whose presidency is commonly called the "Revolution on the March." During his four-year presidency the state was given a constitutionally guaranteed role in economic development and diversification of exports. Legal means were enacted to protect domestic industry; credit institutions were strengthened; a graduated income tax was introduced for the first time, as were taxes on excess profits and patrimony. Labor became a "social obligation" with the special protection of the state. The right to strike was guaranteed, and a series of laws gave unions firmer guarantees in collective bargaining.

Property was to have a social function, and property not being used effectively could be expropriated.

Agrarian reform came along with constitutional change. Law 200 of 1936 stated that presumption of ownership existed in favor of those who occupied the land and made economic use of it. Squatters could not be evicted unless the owner could prove title prior to 1821. All privately owned lands that remained uncultivated for the next ten consecutive years would revert to the public domain.

In education, national expenditures increased fourfold during the López presidency. Primary education, previously the responsibility of municipal and departmental governments, was brought under the national government. Primary education became obligatory, while the national university was strengthened and normal schools were established.[3]

Because of all of these reforms, the López Revolution on the March has been described as the only period of elite-led social reform before 1958. The administration also had the effect of aggravating the divisions between the factions within the two parties. Both Moderate Conservatives and Historical Conservatives reacted to the López reforms; by the time of the 1937 congressional elections, a real and lasting split had occurred within the Liberal party. So serious was the opposition from his own party in the following congressional sessions that López threatened to resign the presidency in May 1937.[4] The leadership of the Moderate Liberals was assumed by Eduardo Santos, owner and editor of the newspaper *El Tiempo*. Santos's followers fought the López programs in congress and, in so doing, many times joined with the Conservatives in defeating the Radical Liberals.[5]

Santos was elected president in 1938. His administration, basically stand pat, tried neither to continue the López reform process nor, very importantly, to rescind it. In many cases, such action was probably not necessary, as policy implementation was never effective.

Although Alfonso López P. returned to the presidency again in 1942, his three years as president in the forties have been called "the reform of the reformer." The revolution did not march again for several reasons: The economic conditions prevalent during World War II were not auspicious for reform; the moderate factions of the two parties had a majority in the congress and could effectively block any López reforms; and opposition groups were able to capitalize on a series of "improprieties" of the López family (although not of the president himself), keeping the president constantly on the defensive.[6] In 1944 López was seized by the garrison in Pasto, and even though the rest of the military supported the constitutional president, López resigned in 1945, a full year before the end of his presidential term. The year was filled by

Alberto Lleras Camargo, who did not try to bring social reform and indeed repressed union strikes that occurred during the interregnum.

The Liberal party split had progressed so far by 1946 that there were two party candidates in the election of that year: Gabriel Turbay, a moderate who received the endorsement of the party convention, and Jorge Eliécer Gaitán, a radical. Gaitán was a mestizo of lower-middle-sector background. He had first come to national attention by condemning the Conservative government for using the army to put down strikes against United Fruit Company in 1928. He had a personal magnetism that some call charisma: one political leader told me that Gaitán had an uncanny ability to cause people, even in the public plaza, to listen to and believe his every word. A Liberal, he was also a populist who made the distinction between the *país político* (the political elite) and the *país nacional* (the real country, with its humble people).[7] What Gaitán might have done if he had become president is open to great speculation; unfortunately he was killed by an assassin's bullet in 1948.

Until six weeks before the presidential election of 1946 there was no Conservative candidate. The last-minute candidacy of Mariano Ospina Pérez led to his election, although he did not receive a majority of the popular vote, and to the end of the short Liberal hegemony. But the stakes of politics had become much greater than before 1930.

The Conservatives in Power and La Violencia

The Mariano Ospina government was, from its beginning until May 21, 1949, a coalition government with the Liberals (see Table 2.1). This coalition formation showed, once again, the abilities of the elites to work together with one hand while with the other encouraging violence of their mass followers.

Yet the Conservative party was never united. Mariano Ospina was a moderate, favored compromise, and worked for coalition government; Laureano Gómez, a Historical Conservative, disagreed on all three issues. Gómez was a reactionary, whom some Colombians believe to have been in large part responsible for the violence described below. In the 1930s, he had been an unabashed supporter of Spain's Francisco Franco: "Spain, marching forward as the sole defender of Christian civilization, leads the Western nations in the reconstruction of empire of *Hispanidad,* and we inscribe our names in the roster of its phalanxes with unutterable satisfaction."[8] Although at one point he stated that "I don't know how to do anything but foul things up,"[9] at times he blamed Jews for the problems of the country and expressed his disdain for majority rule through elections. As president-elect, this "Angry Man of God" stated, "I bless God a thousand and a thousand times for having filled my heart with this burning love for my country and for having made my mind grasp a sublime doctrine. . . . I praise God because he had permitted me to walk through the fires of hatred without allowing my heart to become contaminated by it, and has kept it happy, free from the dark shadows of vengeance, pure, without the dregs of bitterness. . . ."[10] Gómez was elected president in 1949 (the presidential election was legally set earlier than normal), but his term was short; health conditions caused him to turn power over to the *designado*. Neither he nor Ospina had the opportunity to effect changes, as their attentions were monopolized by the growing civil war in the countryside.

With the return of the Conservatives to power, violence on the countryside had started almost immediately, especially in the *departamentos* of Santander, Norte de Santander, and Boyacá. In part this violence was caused by the change of party of the law enforcement officers. Conservative peasants now could do things to Liberals (such as seizing their lands) with impunity. Indeed, it has been reported that in some cases Conservative peasants seized the very same lands in 1946–1947 that Liberal peasants had taken from them in 1930–1931. Another cause was that Conservative party leaders, at least at the local level, were trying to prevent Liberals from voting in the congressional elections of 1947; documentary evidence shows this elite-instigated campaign.[11]

The incipient violence was aggravated by the assassination of Jorge Gaitán in the streets of Bogotá on April 9, 1948. While for the next several days there was considerable violence in the major cities (including the incredibly destructive and life-taking violence in Bogotá, commonly called the *Bogotazo*), *La Violencia*[12] was primarily a rural phenomenon. After the urban violence was over (it lasted but several days in Bogotá), the rural aspect of this nightmare of twentieth-century Colombian history continued, albeit with greater or lesser intensity, until 1964 or 1966.[13]

With the exception of southernmost Nariño, almost all of the Andean part of the country was affected, as were the Orinoco Plains. The Caribbean coast was little affected. At its beginning, *La Violencia* was fought on party lines. Conservatives attacked Liberals, or vice versa (especially after April 9, 1948). The affected group (whose property had been seized and/or destroyed, and some of whose members had been killed and/or raped) fled to isolated parts of the mountains, from which they plotted revenge against members of the other party. This was the "snowball" effect of the violence.

The Conservative governments and their "law enforcement" agencies, the national police and the army, took the Conservative side of the conflict. There was no neutrality of the government. Increasingly, other conflicts became possible because there was no longer effective law enforcement (called a "partial breakdown of the state" by Paul

Oquist[14]). All kinds of latent agrarian conflicts became manifest: over good crop lands, over water rights, over long-standing grudges, and over many other things. While many of these happened to fall along Liberal-Conservative lines (a Conservative village desiring the water of the Liberal village, for example), not all of them did. Almost all of *La Violencia* was between *campesinos*. The cases of *campesino* violence against large landowners were few. From a Marxist point of view, *La Violencia* was based on a "false consciousness." From a Colombian point of view, it was a logical extension of patterns learned during nearly a century of partisan conflict.

La Violencia had certain religious aspects. On the one hand, parish priests refused sacraments to Liberals and at least one bishop threatened to excommunicate people who voted for the Liberal party.[15] On the other hand, Protestants (as few as they were) were persecuted by the Conservatives. While it might have been the case that most Protestants were Liberals, surely most Liberals were not Protestants.

Towards the end of *La Violencia* some "secondary" kinds of violence did occur, in addition to the snowball effect already mentioned. One kind of secondary violence was mere banditry, increasingly coming from a generation of young Colombians who had been socialized to think that violence was a normal way of life. In the 1960s, radical violence also appeared, based on more revolutionary, class-oriented goals. This was late and, although no reliable statistics exist, apparently limited as compared to the other kinds.

At the elite level, the major reason for *La Violencia* was that the stakes had increased so much. The Liberal hegemony, and especially the López reforms, had created a much more important state apparatus. In the context of this enlarged state and sectarianism (the exclusion of the other party from the bureaucratic spoils), winning the presidency became almost a zero-sum game situation. The Conservative leaders tried unsuccessfully to convert their party into a majority one. The Liberal leaders needed to maintain their majority. The conflict escalated to violence, either because the other party had used it first, or it was feared that they soon would use it.

In the end, at least 200,000 Colombian *campesinos* died as a result of *La Violencia*. While the number itself is astounding, the various methods elaborated for one peasant to kill another can only be called macabre.[16]

The Rojas Dictatorship

It was in this context of systemic breakdown that the only military dictatorship of this century took place in Colombia. On June 13, 1953, when Laureano Gómez retook the active presidency from his *designado* and attempted to remove the military commander, Lieutenant General Gustavo Rojas Pinilla, the latter staged a coup that ended the Gómez presidency and, for that matter, "democratic" government until 1958. It should be pointed out that increasingly the Conservative government had not been democratic in any meaningful way; today many Colombians refer to the "Gómez dictatorship."

The Rojas coup was welcomed by members of the elite factions of both political parties, with the obvious exception of the deposed Historical Conservatives. This bipartisan support was to last for several years, although Rojas, who considered himself a Conservative, received his most active support from the moderates of that party.

The Rojas government took immediate steps to bring an end to *La Violencia*. In return for amnesty (and government aid), many of the guerrilla bands ceased fighting. An effort was made to depoliticize the national police by transferring it to the armed forces (it had been part of the ministry of the interior). Press censorship was relaxed; political prisoners were released. In addition, the government started an extensive series of public-works projects and improved the system of credits for small farmers.[17]

The Rojas years were blessed with good prices for coffee on the international market, which gave the government more money to distribute. To an extent, the Colombian dictator patterned himself after Juan Perón of Argentina. Clothing and food were given to poor people, through an organization called the National Secretariat of Social Assistance (SENDAS, Secretarido Nacional de Asistencia Social). The Colombian "Evita" in this effort with the poor was Rojas's daughter, María Eugenia. Motives of Rojas have been debated: Some see Rojas as one who intended to break the power of the traditional party elites; others see him as an opportunist.

Several conclusions seem clear about the Rojas years. The lull in *La Violencia* was only temporary, with the fighting being renewed along the same lines after 1954, although some parts of the country, such as the Llanos Orientales, were spared the renewed violence. Rojas did not carry out any structural realignment of Colombian society, either because he really did not wish to or because he was not able to.

The partisan elite (with the exception of the Moderate Conservatives) became increasingly restive with military government, especially after Rojas called a national convention to draft a new constitution and began talking about a "third force" (a vague idea about a coalition of all groups of society, also patterned after the Perón experience in Argentina) and after it became increasingly clear that Rojas was not going to hold the 1958 presidential election. It is intriguing that, a decade and a half later, Colombian congressmen had more salient memories about the "lack of the normal rules of the political game" during the Rojas years than they did of *La Violencia*.[18]

There were abuses of government that were blamed on Rojas, whether or not he was personally at fault. These included the "Bullring Massacre" on February 5, 1956, when government-hired thugs beat and killed *aficionados* who failed to cheer for Rojas at a Sunday afternoon *corrida*. Press censorship returned.

By early 1957, most organized groups were opposed to Rojas. Leaders of the parties were planning a coalition government; the Catholic church had lost interest in the Rojas experiment. Leaders of most of the economic interest groups, representing the upper levels of Colombian economic life, had supported the labor unions in general strikes.[19] On May 10, 1957, the top military leaders asked Rojas to leave the country. After his departure, these leaders formed a caretaker military junta to govern until August 7, 1958.

THE NATIONAL FRONT, 1958–1974

Origin and Stipulations

While some argue that the National Front government was first inspired by ideas of ex-president López Pumarejo, the specific path of coalition government evolved through two meetings in Spain of former presidents Laureano Gómez and Alberto Lleras, two agreements signed in Bogotá, and a last-minute change caused by Conservative factionalism. At the end, almost all members of the party elites agreed on the coalition.

The first meeting was in Benidorm, Spain, in 1956, while Rojas was still in power. The two leaders there agreed on five points: (1) that common action by the Liberal and Conservative parties was needed to insure the quickest possible return to civilian, democratic government; (2) that both parties must share the blame for the violence and the breakdown of political order; (3) that the military should be returned to the role of protecting the country from external aggression and internal disturbances; (4) that a coalition government or a series of coalition governments would have to be established; and (5) that "Colombia is unfertile land for dictatorship."[20] While the Benidorm rhetoric suggested that both parties were united behind this agreement, such was not the case: the Moderate Conservatives, headed by Mariano Ospina Pérez, were still cooperating with the Rojas government.

This factional dispute between Ospina and Gómez, surely not a new one, continued to prevent agreement. In 1957, the *ospinistas*, after being excluded from the military government for the first time, signed a "Pact of March" with the Liberals. The pact was different in language, but not substance, from the Pact of Benidorm. However, even though followers of Laureano Gómez had written the Pact of March, they later refused to sign it because it appeared to them that the *ospinistas* were asserting themselves too strongly.

The third pact in the series (and the second signed in Spain) was the 1957 one agreed to in Sitges, once again by Gómez and Alberto Lleras. The original goal of ridding Colombia of the military dictatorship had disappeared with the fall of Rojas earlier in the year. The Sitges Pact (once again between Liberals and Gómez Conservatives) stipulated that the first president under the coalition governments would be a Conservative. It of course did not state which Conservative he would be.

Internal conflicts within the Conservative party led to a fourth, and last, pact, that of San Carlos, signed by members of the leadership groups of all party factions. The main stipulation added by San Carlos was that the Conservative candidate would be chosen by the National Congress, which would be elected before the president.

The results of these agreements were then submitted to the people of Colombia, who overwhelmingly approved them as constitutional amendments in a December 1957 plebiscite. Soon afterward, congressional elections were held. The Gómez Conservatives emerged from that election as the largest Conservative faction in congress, hence effectively vetoing the candidacy of Guillermo León Valencia, until then the strongest Conservative presidential candidate. After negotiation, the top faction leaders then agreed that the first president would be a Liberal and that the coalition would be extended from twelve to sixteen years. This final agreement and the other stipulations of the plebiscite were ratified by the congress as a constitutional amendment in 1958.

The National Front (Frente Nacional), as it existed after these byzantine maneuverings, had the following characteristics:

1.   The presidency would alternate every four years between the two traditional parties (*alternación*).
2.   All legislative bodies (National Congress, departmental assemblies, and municipal councils) would be divided equally between the Liberals and Conservatives regardless of the electoral results within a district (*paridad* or parity). Within each of the two traditional parties, seats would be assigned by a list form of proportional representation, as explained in the next section.

3. This same rule of parity would apply to all administrative appointments not under civil service (*carrera administrativa*), such as the presidential cabinet, gubernatorial cabinets, governors, mayors, and any others not chosen through civil service.

4. No parties other than the Liberal and Conservative could take part in elections during the National Front.

5. The civil-service component of the bureaucracy would grow, and indeed cover all but the highest appointments. Partisan criteria would not enter into the selection of civil servants. This was to end the pre–National Front patronage politics, although we shall see that this goal was modified substantially in practice.

6. All legislation had to be passed by a two-thirds majority in the National Congress.

7. A minimum of 10 percent of the national budget had to go to education.

8. Women were given equal political rights. (General Rojas's government had declared female suffrage in 1954, but of course there had been no elections in which to vote.)

In its essence, the National Front was a constitutional mechanism designed to divide *all* national power equally between the two parties. As such it went further than previous coalitions.

Party Politics During the Front

The Colombian party leaders had participated in "political engineering" in order to end military government and return power to the civilians. Competition between the parties was to be ended, so that *La Violencia* (which, it should be remembered, party leaders were instrumental in starting) would end. While the Frente was successful in both of its principal goals, it also had effects that apparently were not anticipated by the leaders, or, if anticipated, were considered less important than ending praetorianism and violence. This section gives an overview of the Frente years, stressing factional competition, immobilism, and the extension of some of the Frente conditions.

Factional Competition. While many thought that such an undemocratic experiment could not last the full sixteen years in Colombia, it did. Two Liberal presidents were elected (Alberto Lleras Camargo, 1958–1962; Carlos Lleras Restrepo, 1966–1970), as were two Conservatives (Guillermo León Valencia, 1962–1966; Misael Pastrana Borrero, 1970–1974). The stipulations of parity were also honored, and the

National Congress, the departmental assemblies, and the more than 800 municipal councils were divided equally between Liberals and Conservatives (although it was reported that some small, rural *municipios* had difficulties in finding a full complement of one party or the other for the councils). The governors were divided equally; the presidential cabinet was also equally divided, with the military minister of defense making such a division of thirteen possible. Various laws were passed to develop a more extensive civil service, all largely unsuccessful. Non-civil-service bureaucrats (the majority) were also divided equally.

Political competition during the Frente years was *factional* competition. While it is certain that factions have always existed within the two parties, the Frente institutional framework allowed factions to flourish as never before. As the president in any election had to be from a certain party, and the legislative bodies were divided equally between the parties regardless of the popular vote, there were no *party* disincentives for *factional* divisions.

As mentioned above, there could be no new political parties during the Frente years. However, "party" was defined in such a way that any group could offer candidates unless it called itself a party. Hence, in addition to the continued divisions between Gómez followers (earlier called Historical Conservatives and Doctrinaire Conservatives and later called Independent Conservatives) and Ospina followers (during the Frente years called Unionista Conservatives) and the "Official" Liberals, two new groups appeared and were allowed to offer candidates. The first was the Revolutionary Liberal Movement (MRL, Movimiento Revolucionario Liberal), which was founded in 1960. It was led by Alfonso López Michelsen (son of the former president). The MRL opposed the National Front and advocated more rapid socioeconomic reforms. It ended in 1967, when López rejoined the "Official" Liberals.

A longer lasting group was the National Popular Alliance (ANAPO, Alianza Nacional Popular), founded in 1961 by former dictator Rojas Pinilla. ANAPO did not declare itself to be a new "political party"; if it had done so, it would not have been able to participate in elections. Rather it was a "movement" that offered both Conservative and Liberal candidates for the National Congress (the Conservatives were notably more successful), a Liberal candidate for president in 1966, and a Conservative one in 1970 (Rojas himself). The apogee of ANAPO was in the 1970 election, in which its Liberal lists garnered 14 percent of the congressional votes and its Conservative lists, 20 percent; Rojas lost the presidential election by only 3 percent of the votes. Indeed there are some who think that the election was stolen from Rojas by governmental fraud in counting the votes. In 1971 ANAPO declared itself to be a new political party, after which its fortunes (and General Rojas's health) declined rapidly. General Rojas died in 1975; for all intents and purposes, his "party" has also died.

In congressional elections extreme factionalism meant a great diversity of choice for the electors. One could vote for a list identified with one of the major factions of the Conservatives or one from the Liberal factions (and ANAPO had both). Furthermore, these factions might offer more than one list, either approved by the departmental leadership (an "official" list) or not having such approval (a "dissident" list). In the 1968 lower-house election, for example, there were 111 Liberal and 108 Conservative lists of candidates in the twenty-three electoral districts (corresponding to *departamentos*). The multiplicity of lists was more pronounced in some *departamentos* than others; the most extreme case was in Nariño, in which there were 10 Liberal and 8 Conservative lists.[21]

In presidential elections, several candidates usually ran. Sometimes these candidates were "illegal," because they were not from the party that constitutionally was to win the presidency that year (for example, Alfonso López M. ran in 1962 as a Liberal MRL candidate). Other times there was little suspense, although there was more than one legal candidate (for example, in 1966 Carlos Lleras Restrepo had only token ANAPO opposition). By far the most competitive election was in 1970, when there were four major Conservative candidates. The National Front candidate was Misael Pastrana, who, in the absence of Conservative agreement, was chosen by the Liberal party convention. Pastrana, himself a Unionist, was opposed by Rojas from ANAPO and by two Independent Conservatives: Evaristo Sourdis and Belisario Betancur. In this four-candidate election, Pastrana won with 36 percent of the national vote.

Despite all of this electoral choice (or perhaps because of it) in congressional elections, Colombian voters abstained in large numbers. The percentage of eligible voters exercising their franchise in congressional elections fell from a high of 60 percent in 1958 to a low of 31 in 1968. In presidential elections the percentages varied from 50 in 1958 to 34 in 1966.[22]

Perhaps more intriguing than this decline in voting (which was not seen in the hotly contested 1970 elections) was the agonizing of the political elite over it. The party leaders had, after all, engineered a system that was to end one form of political behavior—violent acts—and therefore it is not terribly surprising that it ended another kind—voting. In a situation in which the congress and other elected assemblies would be divided equally between the two parties and the presidency would alternate, the only two possible reasons to vote were that one had a sense of civic responsibility or that one favored one faction of a political party more than another. Public-opinion data indicate that the people of Colombia in general never developed an identification with *factions* of the parties. Rather, most stated that they were either Conservatives or Liberals simply. Given these characteristics, the vote had little "marginal benefit," except when there was a protest candidate (such as Rojas in 1970).

Yet there was much concern over the lack of voting. Many, especially groups from the Left, concluded that it was a sign of alienation and that Colombians would, when they could do so after the National Front, vote for more radical alternatives. This has not happened. Further, it can be argued that abstention rates during the National Front were no higher than they had been historically in Colombia, especially when one considers that women, as new voters, were voting less than men.[23]

Immobilism. The founders of the National Front realized that they were engineering a system in which public policymaking would be greatly constrained. As Alberto Lleras said to the people of Colombia in his New Year's address of 1959, the Front would "do everything that the two parties had said should be done, but that each had not allowed the other to do; and not do in sixteen years what one of the parties might want to do, against the will of the other."[24]

It was Alberto Lleras who was most successful in policymaking, largely because his party was united and allied with the larger Conservative faction (the Gómez group for the first two years and the Ospina one for the next two, as electoral fortunes changed). With the growth of factionalism after the Lleras Camargo presidency, policymaking was more and more hampered, especially since a two-thirds vote was needed in the congress.

This immobilism was increased by other characteristics of the Frente governments. The president was a lame duck from almost the beginning of his term. While this is a characteristic in any political system in which immediate reelection is prohibited (for example, for this reason the Mexican president typically waits as long as he can before naming the Revolutionary Institutional party [PRI] candidate), it was particularly acute in a situation in which the president, by constitution, would be followed by a member of the *other* party. It seems reasonable to conclude that at least during the last two years of his term, much more attention was paid to the president's possible successor than to his programs.

The president's cabinet was split into the various factions, including, during the Valencia presidency, both major Conservative groups. The non-civil-service bureaucracy was also split between factions; membership in a *rosca* of one of the factions was more important than technical expertise. A study in 1967 showed that, of the 100,000 government employees, only 3,000 were part of the *carrera administrativa*.[25] The others were divided fifty-fifty between the two parties and in some cases between the various factions of the parties.

Economic interest groups, in this chaotic situation, were very effective in blocking any legislation that disfavored them, because of their contacts with congress people and bureaucrats. To be passed, any meaningful policy needed the consensus of at least the president and his cabinet and of two-thirds of the congress. To be *implemented*, such legislation needed technically proficient bureaucrats whose political interests and family and friendship groups did not prevent such implementation. Given the circumstances, it is not surprising that the National Front governments carried out little in the way of socioeconomic policy. They did, however, have notable successes in some areas, and *La Violencia* was ended.

Constitutional Reform. One of the reactions to the increasing immobilism was the Constitutional Reform of 1968. This ended the two-thirds vote requirement for congressional approval of legislation and strengthened the rulemaking authority of the president to the detriment of the congress.

In addition, the long and complicated reform ended some of the National Front stipulations, while extending some others. This was popularly called the dismantling (*desmonte*) of the National Front, and Article 120, in which the *desmonte* was contained, continues to be important today.

Under the terms of the *desmonte*, cabinet ministries, the offices of governors and mayors, and other administrative positions that were not part of the civil service were to be divided equally between Liberals and Conservatives until August 7, 1978—four years after the termination of the National Front. After that date, according to Article 120, the same offices were to be divided between the parties "in such a way that gives adequate and equitable participation to the major party distinct from that of the president." However, if that nonpresidential party decided not to participate in the executive, the president would be free to name the officials in any way he chose.

Elective legislative bodies would not be divided equally after the National Front. Departmental assemblies and municipal councils became completely competitive in 1970; the National Congress in 1974. Beginning in 1970, new political parties could participate in elections where the rule of parity did not exist and in all elections from 1974 on.

The reform might best be seen as a compromise. Some Colombian political leaders favored an extension of the National Front. Others even talked about the Liberals and Conservatives joining to form a Colombian version of the Mexican PRI. Still others favored a return to complete competition. The final solution was somewhere between the first and

Figure 3.1 Former President Julio César Turbay Ayala (1978–1982)

third of these positions. The debate about Article 120, however, continues today.

THE POST-NATIONAL FRONT PERIOD, 1974-1982

On August 7, 1974, Alfonso López Michelsen was inaugurated as the first freely elected president of Colombia since Laureano Gómez in 1949 (if Gómez could be considered such, given *La Violencia* that prevented full Liberal participation in the 1949 election). López received 56 percent of the national vote in March 1974, thus defeating both

Figure 3.2 President Belisario Betancur (1982–1986)

Alvaro Gómez and María Eugenia Rojas de Moreno Díaz. While López governed under the contraints of Article 120, he did have a Liberal congress behind him.

In 1978, another Liberal, Julio César Turbay Ayala, was elected president, although he barely won over Conservative Belisario Betancur in the elections of that year. Turbay also had the constraints of Article 120 (albeit different than those that López had) and chose to give governmental positions to both major factions of the Conservative party. Turbay had a majority in the National Congress from his party.

In 1982, Conservative Belisario Betancur won the presidency over two Liberal candidates, Alfonso López M. and Luis Carlos Galán. This election showed a clear continuation of the historical pattern of the majority party dividing, thus allowing the minority party to win the presidency. Yet it is also clear that the immobilism of the National Front has not ended with that experiment. This immobilism in its multifaceted nature is discussed in the next chapter.

CONCLUSION

Today Colombia approximates a "democratic" system, at least in comparison to other countries in Latin America. The country is a product of its history, which has reflected regional socioeconomical cleavages. By 1958, it had become clear that Colombia was not ready for complete democracy; indeed, Alberto Lleras had stated as early as 1946 that the only way to end the violence coming with democratic competition was through coalition government.

The coalition government of the National Front did lead to the pacification of the country. Many leaders (and even some academics) feared that the end of the National Front would lead to new outbreaks of violence, so it is understandable that the Constitutional Reform of 1968 included some elements of compromise. Yet compromise implies not doing some things that might be objected to. Given the changes that have occurred in Colombia since 1958, one might ask how much longer the immobilism that comes with compromise can continue.

NOTES

1. Orlando Fals Borda, *Subversión y Cambio Social* (Bogotá: Ediciones Tercer Mundo, 1968), p. 130.

2. This interpretation is given in Bruce Michael Bagley, "Political Power, Public Policy and the State in Colombia: Case Studies of the Urban and Agrarian Reforms during the National Front, 1958–1974," Ph.D. dissertation, University of California, Los Angeles, 1979, pp. 48–60.

3. Robert H. Dix, *Colombia: The Political Dimensions of Change* (New Haven: Yale University Press, 1967), pp. 87–89.

4. Ibid., p. 91.

5. Vernon Lee Fluharty, *Dance of the Millions: Military Rule and the Social Revolution in Colombia 1930–1956*, 2nd ed. (Pittsburgh: University of Pittsburgh Press, 1966), p. 57.

6. John D. Martz, *Colombia: A Contemporary Political Survey* (Chapel Hill: University of North Carolina Press, 1962), pp. 38–41.

7. An excellent biography of Gaitán in English is Richard E. Sharpless, *Gaitán of Colombia: A Political Biography* (Pittsburgh: University of Pittsburgh Press, 1978).

8. Dix, p. 109, quoting from Germán Arciniegas, *The State of Latin America*, trans. Harriet de Onis (New York: Alfred A. Knopf, 1952), p. 163.

9. Alexander W. Wilde, "Conversations among Gentlemen: Oligarchical Democracy in Colombia," in Juan J. Linz and Alfred Stepan, eds., *The Breakdown of Democratic Regimes: Latin America* (Baltimore: The Johns Hopkins University Press, 1978), p. 56, quoting Augusto Ramírez Moreno, *La crisis del partido conservador* (Bogotá: n.p., 1937), p. 25.

10. Martz, pp. 96–97, quoting Arciniegas, p. 176.

11. The most complete Colombian study, including documents that show this elite instigation, is Germán Guzmán Campos, Orlando Fals Borda, and Eduardo Umaña Luna, *La Violencia en Colombia*, 2 vols. (Bogotá: Ediciones Tercer Mundo, 1962, 1964).

12. While in Spanish the term *la violencia* means simply "the violence," for most Colombians the two words refer specifically to the partisan violence discussed in this section. There is, however, considerable disagreement about when it began (some say 1946, others 1948) and, to a lesser degree, when it ended.

13. Based on the number of deaths per year, Paul Oquist, *Violence, Conflict, and Politics in Colombia* (New York: Academic Press, 1980), p. 9, argues that 1966 was the last year of the violence begun in 1946.

14. Ibid., Chapter 5.

15. Guzmán, Fals Borda, and Umaña, vol. 1, pp. 270–274.

16. The first volume of the Guzmán, Fals Borda, and Umaña study included photographs of these various methods of killing, including, for example, the *corte de franela* ("undershirt cut"). However, in some of the copies of this book in U.S. libraries, this "visual aid" has been removed.

17. Dix, pp. 117–118.

18. Harvey F. Kline, "Selección de Candidatos" in Gary Hoskin, Francisco Leal, Harvey Kline, Dora Rothlisberger, and Armando Borrero, *Estudio del Comportamiento en Colombia* (Bogotá: Editorial Universidad de los Andes, 1975), p. 173.

19. Jonathan Hartlyn, "Interest Groups and Political Conflict in Colombia: A Retrospective and Prospective View," Paper given at the U.S. State Department Conference on Colombia, November 9, 1981, p. 4.

20. Miles Wendell Williams, "El Frente Nacional: Colombia's Experiment in Controlled Democracy," Ph.D. dissertation, Vanderbilt University, 1972, p. 78, quoting from Guillermo Hernández Rodríguez, *La Alternación ante el Pueblo como Constituyente Primario* (Bogotá: n.p., 1962), pp. 12–16.

21. Harvey F. Kline, "The Cohesion of Political Parties in the Colombian Congress: A Case Study of the 1968 Session," Ph.D. dissertation, University of Texas, 1970, p. 68.

22. Rodrigo Losada, "Electoral Participation," in R. Albert Berry, Ronald G. Hellman, and Mauricio Solaún, eds., *Politics of Compromise: Coalition Gov-*

ernment in Colombia (New Brunswick, N.J.: Transaction Books, 1980), pp. 90, 95.

23. Ibid., p. 90.

24. Alberto Lleras Camargo, *Sus Mejores Páginas* (Bogotá: n.p., n.d.), p. 266.

25. Hartlyn, p. 25. He adds that, by 1976, only 13,000 people had joined the *carrera administrativa*.

4

Government and Politics

The previous chapters have described the givens—natural, socio-economic, and historical—of Colombia. This chapter describes the governmental and political situation as of mid-1982. To that end, I will discuss the formal structure and informal structure of government and the major power groups of the society.

GOVERNMENT STRUCTURE: FORMAL AND INFORMAL

It should be stressed that what documents say exists in Colombian politics, on the one hand, and what really exists, on the other, are quite often two different things. As in many Latin American countries, constitutions are not always followed to the letter and laws are not carried out—either because there is no bureaucratic capability to do so or because there never was any intention to. This contradiction, which makes the study much more difficult, is seen repeatedly. Just one small case might make the point. In 1981, I heard the minister of health say on television that it was illegal to sell medicine without a physician's prescription. But that very morning, I had bought a prescription drug without seeing a doctor. Should such an example seem unimportant, it is a thesis of this section that such disparity between the formal and informal exists at all levels of law.

THE EXECUTIVE BRANCH

Within the national government, the executive branch is the strongest. Within that branch, the president is the one person with the most power. These concentrations of power have become more and more the case in recent years.

Presidential Powers

The president is elected for a four-year term and is not eligible for immediate reelection. Only a plurality is needed for election. There is no vice president, but rather a designate (*designado*) who takes over upon the death, the resignation, or the temporary incapacitation of the president, and (on occasion, but not always) when the president leaves the country. The *designado* is elected for a two-year term by the congress.

Formal Powers. The formal powers of the president are impressive. He names and removes (without congressional concurrence) cabinet officials, heads of government agencies, governors of the *departamentos*, and other public officials. He is charged with maintaining national security, declaring war (with the permission of the senate, unless foreign aggression makes such impossible), and negotiating foreign treaties. He can direct war operations, when necessary, as the commander of the armed forces. His formal powers in the day-to-day workings of the government are wide sweeping, including those of conferring military degrees and directing the military; collecting taxes; regulating, directing, and inspecting national public education; negotiating contracts for public works; organizing public credit; exercising the inspection of banks and corporations; and preserving public order.

State of Siege. If the above powers (which do not include all that the constitution lists) are not impressive enough, the president—either because of international war or internal disturbances—can declare a "state of siege." All cabinet ministers must approve this declaration (but of course all were named by, and can be removed by, the chief executive). During the state of siege, the president rules by decree (which also must be approved by all the ministers). These decrees may not overturn existing laws, but may suspend them. Congress continues to meet as it normally would, and all decrees promulgated must be sent the following day to the supreme court, which can declare that they are unconstitutional.

State of Emergency. Further, in the case of economic crisis, the president can declare a "state of emergency." This is similar to the state of siege, but with the stipulation that the decrees issued can deal only with the specific situation that led to the declaration of the state of emergency. It can last a maximum of ninety days a year.

These provisions of the constitution are extremely important in understanding recent Colombian politics. There has been an almost constant state of siege or state of emergency since 1949. Those coming from internal disturbances have been more common, although Alfonso López Michelsen began his presidency in 1974 by declaring an economic emergency and, a few months after it ended, a state of siege. However, the congress does continue to meet as scheduled and the supreme court does, on occasion, declare decrees to be unconstitutional. Two recent examples show that the Colombian state of siege is not as complete as that of some Latin American countries.

The López Michelsen state of siege was still in force when Julio César Turbay became president in August 1978. The following month Turbay, using his decree power, promulgated a Security Statute (Estatuto de Seguridad), which remained in force until the president rescinded it in July 1982. Based on general insecurity, crime, terrorism, and kidnapping, the statute proclaimed stiffer prison sentences for crimes such as kidnapping; leadership and membership in subversive bands; disruption of public order; bribery; inciting riot; illegally occupying public offices; and manufacturing, distributing, transporting, and carrying firearms, ammunitions, or explosives. Further, it was prohibited to broadcast, by television or radio, any declaration, communiqué, or commentary about public order, illegal strikes, or any other news story that might incite disorder. All individuals arrested for these crimes (other than broadcasting and those having to do with firearms, ammunition, and explosives) were tried by courts-martial.

While these stipulations were far reaching, it is important to note that the supreme court and the congress constrained them *to a degree.* The supreme court found certain parts of the Estatuto to be unconstitutional: for example, the stipulation that "subversive propaganda" could not be passed out in government offices. In 1981, the court ruled that the new Legal Code, passed by the congress the previous year, superseded the sentences stated in the Estatuto. Yet neither governmental branch addressed the basic questions of courts-martial and the lack of the right of bail.

In addition to the decree power during states of siege, a Colombian president has the power to promulgate regulations that interpret the laws passed by the congress. Using these *decretos reglamentarios,* the president puts specific stipulations to the very general "framework laws" that the legislative body passes. The president, however, must be careful not to change those laws. Any Colombian can initiate a law suit that might lead to the supreme court's overturning all or part of such regulatory decrees.

Restrictions on Presidential Powers

As impressive as these formal powers are (and they surely do make the Colombian president *potentially* the most powerful person in the government), one should not necessarily conclude that the president as an individual always has complete power, even if he wants it. While power flows through the presidency, whether the individual president is merely a "chief clerk" or an actual shaper of policy depends on a variety of factors.

In the first place, a Colombian president's days are only twenty-four hours long. There is no way that one person *could do* everything that the president *can do*—especially when ceremonial duties all over the country are added to the powers already enumerated. By necessity, then, some power must be delegated to cabinet ministers. Other powers, by law, have been given to decentralized institutes (*institutos decentralizados*).

The Cabinet. The president's cabinet is, by law, a coalition one. This sometimes means that a politician who was in opposition to legislation proposed by the president one year may be in the cabinet the next (this politician being a leader in one of the factions of the "second largest party"). For example, in 1979 Senator Felio Andrade led the opposition to the Turbay administration's Coal Law. In 1980–1981, Andrade was minister of justice in the Turbay cabinet. Such changing sands of coalition formation must place limits on the president's power.

The relationship between the president and the cabinet is a matter of some controversy. Some stress that an individual president, if he has the inclination, can at times personally (or along with a few ministers) make policy changes. Hence it is said that Carlos Lleras Restrepo was able to force a renegotiation of oil contracts in the Putumayo region, despite multinational corporation (MNC) recalcitrance.[1] Others stress that the president has a term much longer than the ministers. Alfonso López, for example, had five ministers of mines and energy in four years and Turbay three, through his first three years. As one former minister told me, "This is just one of the givens of Colombian politics; you have to work within it."[2] What is not completely clear, however, is whether this ministerial turnover is because of policy disagreements or because of other factors (such as the necessities of coalition formation and the desire of ministers to move on to elected political office).

This rapid turnover might have several meanings. Many suggest today that although "minor" ministers come and go with great rapidity, there are two "super ministers"—the minister of the treasury (*hacienda*) and the minister of defense. Any action having to do with the allocation of financial resources would have to be approved by the relevant minor minister and the super minister of *hacienda*. Therefore, it is argued, rapid turnover in minor ministries is not so important as long as there is stability in the *hacienda* portfolio.[3]

Further, some of the turnover comes when certain individuals change from one post to another in high levels of the administration. It was not a sign of significant change, for example, when Jaime García Parra went from being minister of mines to minister of *hacienda*.

Even if the president and the ministers agree on policy within an area, there are societal constraints to their power. The president and the ministers cannot unilaterally make public policy if the interests of organized economic interest groups are involved and if the policy changes must be made through laws that pass through the National Congress, rather than through executive implementation of previous laws. At times ministers (with or without presidential approval) apparently have considerable "initiative space," that is, the power to suggest changes without constraint.[4] How much of this initiative space is "decision space," however, depends on the strength of the affected interests.

There are further potential constraints on the president's power within the executive branch itself. These come from four areas: the bureaucracy, the decentralized institutes, the National Planning Department (DNP, Departamento Nacional de Planeación), and the National Council of Economic and Social Policy (CONPES, Concejo Nacional de Política Económica y Social).

The Bureaucracy. The growth of the Colombian bureaucracy in recent decades has been almost exponential. As early as the Liberal hegemony (1930–1946), the bureaucracy began growing as the state took on more responsibilities. During the Santos administration, the first "decentralized institute" was founded. The National Front put even more emphasis on government's role in the society and the economy, and the rate of growth increased. Indeed, some even argue that *parity* came only by adding new bureaucrats and never by firing any.

The bureaucratic job is highly sought. Although salaries are not extremely high, the jobs are white-collar and give the prestige of being in the "mental sector." Since *at most* 15 percent of the bureaucrats are products of the civil service (*carrera administrativa*), party or faction loyalty is more important than technical expertise in obtaining a bureaucratic position. As Article 120 is still in force for non-career-service bureaucrats, the second party is always assured of an "adequate and equitable" participation. However, it appears that few bureaucrats are ever fired when governing coalitions change; the result is a badly paid group of bureaucrats, whose work conditions are terrible and whose patronage ties become weakened or disappear. It is little wonder that they become dissatisfied and radicalized.

Decentralized Institutes. One method of avoiding the problems of patronage politics is the use of decentralized institutes. The earliest of these, the Industrial Promotion Institute (IFI, Instituto de Fomento Industrial) was established in 1940. The institutes are "under the tutelage" of a ministry, although the exact meaning of this is not always clear. Table 4.1 lists some of the major institutes; there are many others. The

TABLE 4.1
Major Institutos Decentralizados, 1978

Tutelary Ministry	Acronym/ Title	Function
Public Works and Transportation	INTRA	Transportation
	COLPUERTOS	Ports
	FFCC	Railroads
Communications	ADPOSTAL	Mail
	TELECOM	Telephone, telegraph
	INRAVISION	Radio, television
Education	COLCIENCIAS	Science
	COLCULTURA	Culture
	COLDEPORTES	Sports
	ICFES	University Education
Economic Development	INCOMEX	Foreign commerce
	ICT	Housing Credit
	PROEXPO	Exports
	IFI	Industrial Promotion
Mines and Energy	INGEOMINAS	Geological Investigations
	ICEL	Electricity
	ECOMINAS	Mines
	ECOPETROL	Petroleum
	CARBOCOL	Coal
Labor and Social Security	ICBF	Welfare
	ICSS	Social Security
	SENA	Technical Education
Agriculture	INCORA	Agrarian Reform
	INDERENA	Renewal Resources, Environment
	HIMAT	Water Resources, Meteorology
	Caja Agraria	Credit
	Banco Ganadero	Credit
Treasury and Public Credit	Banco Central Hipotecario	Mortgages
	Banco de la República	Central Bank

"tutelage" means that the respective minister usually is a member of the board of directors of the institute and hence plays a role in policy. Yet ministers come and go, while the institutes remain. One case is the Colombian Petroleum Enterprise (ECOPETROL, Empresa Colombiana de Petróleos) founded in 1951. While there have been eight ministers of mines since 1974, ECOPETROL has had two directors. Indeed, it is reported that ECOPETROL has considerable independence in its internal policy.[5] Yet others would stress that the minister of mines (and the president) have an important role in naming the director of ECOPETROL.

It seems safe to conclude that the *institutos decentralizados* are not completely decentralized from the patronage politics. During the Turbay years, it was reported that the head of ECOPETROL was the son of a friend of the president and that he had received the position over presumably more able candidates nominated to the president by the ministers of mines and *hacienda*. But the staff of the institutes do tend to be less part of the political patronage game than their counterparts in the bureaucracy directly under the ministries. They also are paid higher salaries than the regular bureaucrats (although not so high that private business—both Colombian and MNC—cannot offer them better).

Finally it is important to point out that the institutes receive *more* of the national budget each year than the ministries do. They do have more independence in policy and, in the absence of a forceful minister who can coordinate (which is to say, most of the time), are likely to carry out their programs without concern about overall national interest and without coordination with other institutes. Research has shown this to be the case in energy, water resource development, and food production, and it is likely to be the case elsewhere as well.

Coordinating Groups. For this reason, governments of the National Front and since have sought a way of coordinating policy through what today are called the National Planning Department (DNP) and the National Council of Social and Economic Policy (CONPES). The first attempt was in 1958, when a National Council of Economic Policy and Planning was established. Made up of the president and four additional members (two named by the president, one by the senate, and one by the house of representatives), this council was to study and coordinate economic policies, project general development plans, and present governmental indications to the private sector.[6]

The second attempt was in 1963, when the National Council of Economic Policy was created. The functions of the council were changed to concentrate on plan approval and determination of specific policy measures to implement the plans. Its membership was as follows: the president (chairman); the ministers of *hacienda*, development, agriculture, and public works; the head of the planning department; the manager of the Banco de la República; and the manager of the National Federation of Coffee Growers.

Finally, in 1968, the council was expanded (and given its current name): added were the ministers of foreign relations and of labor and the director of the Foreign Trade Institute (INCOMEX, Instituto Colombiano de Comercio Exterior). Moreover, other people from technical public organizations were permitted to attend council meetings when invited by the president. The council was assigned four basic functions: (1) to recommend general economic policies as guides for plans, (2) to study and evaluate plans submitted by the planning department, (3) to study periodic reports prepared by the secretary general of the National Planning Department, and (4) to coordinate economic policies and activities of the state.

The National Planning Department by 1968 had evolved to such a point that it had an established staff. The reform of that year gave it impressive powers (at least on paper). These were the power to:

1. prescribe norms for the establishment and operation of departmental, municipal, and other sectoral offices
2. provide technical assistance to these offices
3. prepare development plans and present them to the CONPES
4. evaluate and seek adjustments during plan execution
5. study sectoral, regional, and local plans, and generate them into general development plans
6. make proposals regarding economic policies and submit special studies to the CONPES
7. coordinate the preparation of plans with other public institutions
8. submit to the president and the congress reports on plan execution.

If the Planning Department and the CONPES worked in practice as the formal rules state they do, the two organizations would represent rationality in planning and continuity from one presidency to the next. This also would mean that the coordinating groups would constrain the power of any president. Yet neither the Planning Department nor the CONPES has been an effective coordinator. Several reasons might be highlighted. For one thing, the commitment to planning has varied from one presidency to another. Politically—in a very patronage-oriented administration such as that of President Turbay—it was easier to allow the *institutos decentralizados* to go their own way. For another thing, the officials of the National Planning Department tend to have short tenures in office: they are often hired away by private businesses that can offer better salaries.

It seems reasonable to conclude that the Colombian system—which is supposed to be one of "indicative planning" for the private sector and of obligatory planning for the public one—is more one of indicative planning for the public sector and no planning for the private sector. Lack of coordination is a chronic problem in the public sector; it is likely to continue.

THE NATIONAL CONGRESS AND THE SUPREME COURT

Although secondary in power, both the National Congress and the supreme court do have some authority. The congress is an effective arena in which legislation can be modified or indeed completely blocked; few laws of importance originate in the legislative body, however.

The Legislative Branch

The electoral district for the congress is the *departamento*. Each *departamento* has two senators, plus an additional one for each 200,000 inhabitants. Likewise, the *departamento* has two members of the lower house (Cámara de Representantes), plus an additional one for each 100,000 people. Terms in both houses are four years.

The electoral system used for both houses is a proportional-representation list system, in which voters vote for the entire list. If a list has the right to two senators (for example), the first two on the list are elected. Further, both principal members (*principales*) and alternates (*suplentes*) are elected. If any *principal* decides not to attend the congress, the first *suplente* takes his or her place. To further complicate matters, the particular variant of the list system (like the former *ley del lema* in Uruguay) encourages multiple lists. If any list receives less than one-half of the electoral quotient (defined as the total number of votes divided by the number of seats), those votes are assigned to the list with the same label that received the most votes.

As a result of these structures (which were engineered, no doubt, because of the recurring factionalism in Colombian politics), the congress is the *país político* par excellence. Today one finds in the congress Turbay Liberals, Lleras Liberals, Gómez Conservatives, Betancur Conservatives, Pastrana Conservatives, members of ANAPO, Communists, and others. Although most consider Colombia to be a two-party system, the congress functions more like a multiparty one. On any issue the "natural leaders" of the factions have some clout. Weak followers will follow the lead of the *jefe*, hoping that such loyalty will get them a high position (*renglón*) on the list the next time; followers who have some independent basis of support might be more rebellious.

Coalitions tend to be transitory and change from year to year. To take but one recent case, coal policy, is instructive. In 1979 the Turbay Liberals and Pastrana Conservatives favored the Coal Law; opposition was led by the Gómez Conservatives. In the 1981 debate on the Cerrejón contract (see Chapter 5), the Lleras Liberals and Unionist Conservatives (with mixed signals, albeit) opposed the Turbay Liberals and the Gómez Conservatives. Little wonder that the congress has become less and less of a public policymaking branch.

Indeed, the 1968 constitutional reform explicitly took power from the congress. The president can declare any initiative to be "urgent," hence giving the congress only thirty days to defeat it. All economic bills have to originate in the administration. The major contribution to planning by the congress is the Comisión del Plan (Plan Commission), a bicameral body that met for the first time thirteen years after the constitution established it!

Yet the congress does convene on July 20 each year and has regular sessions of 150 days. If work is not finished, presidents can call "extraordinary sessions," during which only executive proposals can be considered. Ministers are questioned on the floor of the two houses (and can be cited if they fail to attend). As compared with other Latin American legislatures, then, the Colombian one is impressive.

The Judicial Branch

The judicial branch is headed by a supreme court of justice. It has a varying number of members (as established by law), who serve eight-year terms and are elected by the court itself. The court can (and does) rule on the legality of presidential decrees. It also can judge officials who have been impeached by the senate and can rule on the constitutionality of laws passed by the congress.

Perhaps the most notable exercise of power by the supreme court in recent years was the October 1981 declaration that the Constitutional Reform of 1979 (which President Turbay had called the "most important" reform of the century) was unconstitutional. This decision was based on procedural irregularities during the 1979 sessions of the congress. The Turbay administration reacted angrily. The court was accused of making the decision on political grounds; it also was argued that the court had to make such a decision by a three-fifths vote. The attacks were so strong that one member of the court, Manuel Gaona, stated that "A government of General Landazábal would be preferable to a government of señor Turbay."[7] In the end, although there was apparently some fear of a military intervention during the recriminations between the president and the court, there was none, and the court's ruling stood. As a result, some economic reforms were left without legal basis, the new system of appointing judges was ended, and the automatic cost-of-living escalation factor for government salaries also ended.

REGIONAL AND LOCAL GOVERNMENT

Colombia is divided into twenty-four *departamentos* (Caquetá became the twenty-fourth in January 1982) and into *intendencias* and *comisarías*. The latter divisions are areas of small population, particularly in the Amazon and Orinoco areas. Each *departamento* has a governor, named and removed by the president, and a departmental assembly (*asamblea departamental*). The assembly is elective, through a proportional-representation list system similar to that of the congress. The *asamblea* is extremely secondary in power to the governor.

Each of the more than 900 *municipios* has a mayor (*alcalde*) named by the governor of the respective department (with the exception of the mayor of Bogotá, who is named by the president). Each *municipio* also has a council (*concejo*) elected through the proportional-representation list system. The *concejo* is secondary in power to the *alcalde*.

Both departmental and municipal government are weak as compared to the national government. Although there are some bureaucracies at those levels, most Colombian bureaucrats are part of the national government. Tax revenues for the *departamento* and *municipio* governments are limited. *Departamentos* receive most of their revenues from the liquor monopolies and lotteries that each has; municipalities are increasingly using property taxes (and for some time have been collecting fees for provision of municipal services such as garbage removal and water).

Individual politicians can hold posts in all three levels of legislatures at the same time: congress, *asamblea*, and *concejo*. The National Congress typically grinds to a halt when the *asambleas* begin their short sessions. Further, the lack of a residency requirement might mean that a politician represents one area of the country in the congress, is on the *concejo* of a city, and is on the *asamblea* in yet another area of the country. This lack of residency requirement also applies to the appointive positions of governor and mayor.

PARTIES, GROUPS, AND INFORMAL DYNAMICS

Three conclusions emerge from an analysis of organized groups in Colombian society. First, those groups that are organized effectively tend to come from the upper socioeconomic levels of society. Labor is less organized, and the very poor (both urban and rural) hardly at all. Second, the government has the right (apparently not often used) to withhold necessary legal recognition (*personería jurídica*, or juridical personality). Without governmental granting of this status, no group can legally exist. Third (and quite related), the Colombian state does not approach the organic model to the degree that some Latin American countries do, such as Brazil or Mexico.

POLITICAL PARTIES

Political parties in Colombia have always been elitist instruments of control. Leadership almost always has come from the highest socioeconomic groups, whether or not one wishes to call this an *oligarquía* as the Colombians themselves do. Some people, believing that "anyone can be president," draw attention to presidents from humble origins, such as Marco Fidel Suárez, Conservative president during the 1920s, who was born in a grass hut, the illegitimate son of a washerwoman. While these facts about Suárez are historically accurate, it is not mentioned that by the time of his political career, he had married into a traditional family.[8] While the myth that "anyone can be president" will gain apparent substantiation from the 1982 election of Belisario Betancur (one of twenty-two children of an illiterate peasant), the facts of elite control of the parties will remain.

While parties have been effective linkages from the top down (thus explaining the ability to initiate civil war), the reverse has not been the case: the parties do not participate effectively in the "interest aggregation" function. This is the case today and has been so historically. When the party elites turn to new social groups, some of the aspirations of those groups are met; yet the key goal is to capture and control those emergent groups.

Factionalism

Today it is largely a reification to talk of Liberal and Conservative parties. While there is once again electoral conflict between the two traditional parties, and it is important (at least at the personal level of elite members) which party won the presidency in 1982, the more "real" conflicts in elite politics are between the various factions of the two parties. These factional disputes—with name calling and various kinds of accusations—take up more space in the major Bogotá newspapers than the traditional Liberal-Conservative conflicts. In a series of lectures given by the presidential "precandidates" (those trying to obtain the nomination from the respective party conventions) in 1981 at the Universidad de los Andes in Bogotá, two of the three precandidates stated that there were no longer ideological differences between the two parties. Only Augusto Espinosa (Liberal) thought that differences remained; both Alberto Santofimio (Liberal) and Belisario Betancur (Conservative) thought that there were none. Betancur stated it most poetically, "The difference is that the color of the Conservative party is blue, the color of the Virgin Mary. The Liberal color is red, color of the Sacred Heart of Jesus."[9]

Only one faction of a party, in the recent year when I was in Bogotá, made an attempt to present a different ideological program: Nuevo Liberalismo, a movement founded by Luis Carlos Galán and others. While Nuevo Liberalismo produced a program based on twelve major points, it is of note that Galán himself is a protégé of Carlos Lleras Restrepo and hence, to a certain degree, is a product of the cliental system of *roscas*. The "ideology" proclaimed in June 1981 included the following major points:

1. the necessity of radically transforming the congress
2. the regulation and publicity of financial sources of candidates
3. the "relief" (*relevo*) of the political oligarchy that dominates the congress
4. the intervention of the state in the growth of the large cities
5. defense of human rights
6. control of monopolies and oligopolies
7. the revision of all contracts in petroleum, coal, uranium, and other natural resources
8. the reorganization of the state so that it can defend national sovereignty in the face of the financial and technological power of large foreign companies
9. the cultural identity and the recuperation of and diffusion of "the values which explain the national conscience"
10. the defense of the rights of the indigenous populations
11. television reform
12. support of the spirit of progressive unionism.[10]

Realignment

Some argue that the party elites are in the process of realigning. It has been suggested that new political parties might emerge or that more permanent coalitions between progressive Liberals (Galán) and Conservatives (Betancur) might come from the process. Others suggest that what is going on today is not unlike earlier party-elite behavior. While no firm conclusions can be reached at this time, the 1982 presidential campaign is instructive. After the last-moment entry of

Alfonso López Michelsen as a precandidate (and his receiving the Liberal nomination), Luis Carlos Galán announced his candidacy without the party imprimatur. Galán quickly received the endorsement of Carlos Lleras and of a leading Bogotá daily, El Espectador. This Liberal behavior, reminiscent of the 1946 election, allowed the Conservatives to offer a single candidate, Belisario Betancur, for the May 30 election. The Liberals were unable to reach an agreement that the congressional elections (held in March) would serve as a kind of "primary," even though such an agreement had been reached in 1978 in similar circumstances. Nor did a Liberal candidate drop out after the congressional elections, even though the congressional lists identified with López won 46 percent of the vote, while the Galán lists won only 11 percent. In the end, there were three candidates in the May 30 elections. The Liberal party received a majority of the votes, but they were split between López (40 percent) and Galán (12 percent). Belisario Betancur won the presidency with 47 percent of the more than 7 million votes cast. He became president on August 7 and is the first Conservative elected in a competitive election between the two traditional parties since Mariano Ospina in 1946.

While there is the possibility of change at the party-elite level, such is also the case at the mass level. Recent public-opinion survey studies show that only 64 percent of the respondents in Bogotá identified with one of the two traditional parties in 1978 (46 percent Liberal and 18 percent Conservative), as compared with 73 percent in 1974 and 80 percent in 1970.[11] While it is clearly not proper to project this tendency in a linear fashion or to conclude that similar figures and tendencies exist in other cities or the countryside, one might argue that there is a decrease in the degree and intensity of psychological identification with the two traditional parties. In the 1982 presidential election, for example, no doubt many people who considered themselves "Liberals" voted for the Conservative Betancur, even though López had made some attempts to "wave the bloody flag" of party loyalty, reminding (sometimes not so subtly) members of his party of La Violencia.

There are probably two reasons for this change of party identification. First, Colombians are now primarily urban inhabitants. As a result, they have neither the traditional patron-client relationships on which party loyalty had been based in part nor the same problems. Second, there has been—thanks to the National Front—no partisan violence since the mid-1960s. In a period of rapid population growth, this means that almost one-half of the Colombians living today have not lived during a period of partisan violence. While no doubt some of them heard stories about the malevolent behavior of the other party from their parents, these tales probably lose force as the years go by.

Minor Parties

There are other parties in Colombia today. The oldest is the Colombian Communist party (PCC, Partido Comunista Colombiano), which has existed for over fifty years. While at times it has been illegal, today it legally offers candidates and occasionally elects congresspeople.

ANAPO still exists and is split into two groups. María Eugenia Rojas de Moreno Díaz heads one faction (although with little electoral success). Another group calls itself ANAPO-FUP (Alianza Nacional Popular–Frente Unido del Pueblo or National Popular Alliance–Peoples United Front) and considers itself radical. (I was struck, when visiting their offices, that on one wall was a photograph of General Rojas and on another, one of Che Guevara.) Several congresspeople have been elected in recent years by ANAPO-FUP.

Finally, there are various radical parties. Most often these radical parties have not been able to agree on a single presidential candidate, and when they do, the vote received is small, always less than 10 percent. In 1974, the United Leftist congressional lists received 7 percent of the vote. In 1982, Gerardo Molina, as a coalition candidate of the Communists and various radical groups, received only 1 percent of the presidential vote.

Because of historical patterns and the inability of the Left to unite (and its unpopularity with voters), it seems safest to conclude that the traditional parties will continue to win presidential, and most congressional, elections. Yet there is always the possibility that events, either inside the country or outside it, might lead to dramatic changes.

IMPORTANT GROUPS

Economic Interest Groups

The traditional parties plus a few economic interest groups are the most powerful force in Colombia today (some even suggest that the economic groups are of greater importance than the parties). All economic sectors of the upper- and middle-income groups are organized. But the most powerful seem to be those "peak" organizations of economic activities, the National Federation of Coffee Growers and a few other producer associations.[12]

Most probably the most powerful of the *gremios* (the economic interest groups) is the National Association of Industrialists (ANDI, Asociación Nacional de Industriales). Although there is no overall peak organization of all producer associations, ANDI approximates one as it includes not only the large industrialists, but also firms from the

TABLE 4.2
Major Producer Associations

Acronym	Sector
ANDI	Industry (Large)
ACOPI	Industry (Small and Medium)
SAC	Agriculture
FEDECAFE	Coffee
FEDEGAN	Livestock Raisers
FENALCO	Commerce
CONFCAMARAS	Commerce
ASOBANCARIA	Banking
ANIF	Banking and Finance
CAMACOL	Construction
FASECOLDA	Insurance

agribusiness, insurance, financial, and commercial sectors. Founded in 1944, ANDI is the leading advocate of free enterprise in Colombia and has important roots in the Medellín industrialists. It is powerful because of its wealth and social prestige, the common overlapping of membership of the group with that of the government, and the fact that industrialization has been a major goal of almost all Colombian presidents during the last half century. ANDI tends to oppose anything that might negatively affect the private sector, but historically has supported the government when there is opposition to the basic system of government.

Other major producer associations are shown in Table 4.2. All come from the upper sector; all seek to maintain the status quo. Some generalizations about their political behavior can be made. Most elements of the private sector have been antimilitary, and some of the organizations were important in the 1957 fall of Rojas Pinilla. Although they might sometimes disagree with the policy of a government, they have supported the political regime, whether it was the National Front or the "democratic" system since the end of the front. The associations tend to react to governmental policy, rather than initiating policy. With the growth of the executive branch—both in the ministries and the decentralized institutes—the associations have developed strong ties with that branch. This does not mean, however, that they will not use connections within the congress if such is the preferable way to block governmental policy.

One very special producer association is the National Federation of Coffee Growers (FEDECAFE, Federación Nacional de Cafeteros). Founded in 1927, this association is open to any person interested in developing the coffee industry, but is dominated by the large coffee growers. The federation collects various taxes on coffee and has used its wealth to invest in banks and shipping. It has a close relationship with the government, given the importance of coffee to economic policy. One big difference between Colombia and other Latin American countries is the degree of "privatization" of certain key functions. Nowhere else would a legally private organization be allowed to do what FEDECAFE does; the governments would do it directly.[13]

With the lack of differentiation of the political parties and their factions, interest articulation and aggregation increasingly have been done by the *gremios* (who have made efforts to be bipartisan) and by the church and the military. The *gremios* most recently (although not for the first time) stated the position of some of them when, in April 1981, the "Frente Gremial" published an analysis of Colombian problems. Composed of the presidents of ANDI, the Colombian Chamber of Construction (CAMACOL), the Colombian Federation of Metallurgical Industries (FEDEMETAL), the National Federation of Merchants (FENALCO), and the National Association of Financial Institutions (ANIF), the frente did not limit itself to issues directly affecting the economic activities of the *gremios*. Rather, general issues such as inflation, lack of housing for the poor, and the minimum wage were considered and solutions proposed. In so doing, the frente was aggregating interests in a way that it is supposed that political parties do.

While this activity of the Frente Gremial was not well received by President Turbay, one should not therefore discount the power of the *gremios*. As will be shown in Chapter 5, these economic interest groups have considerable power in public policymaking.

A new economic group, whose importance is hard to estimate, is the illicit drug industry. Called the *mafia* by Colombians, the assumption quite often is that foreign organized crime, particularly from the United States, is also involved. Even if this is true, the drug industry did hold a national convention secretly in December 1981, which 223 drug-gang bosses attended. One notable "accomplishment" of the meeting was the creation of a death squad called MAS (Muerte a Secuestradores or

Death to Kidnappers). The *mafiosos* pledged US$7.5 million to the squad, whose goal is to kill all kidnappers and to end the guerrilla practice of kidnapping people, including the "honest, hard working drug gang bosses," for ransom to finance their subversive activities.[14]

Colombians now assume that the gang leaders are "laundering" their money in legitimate industries and sending their children to the best schools. Surely this is a group (given the economic importance of the drug traffic) that would be included in any discussion of economic groups, although it does not always fit into generalizations about group behavior in Colombia.

Labor Unions

Organized labor is a weak political force in Colombia. In part this is because of the small percentage of the work force that is unionized. Divisions among labor federations, some of which are along traditional political party lines, are another cause.

The first national labor federation was the Confederation of Colombian Workers (CTC, Confederación de Trabajadores Colombianos), founded in 1936 during the first administration of Alfonso López Pumarejo (the "Revolution on the March") and with his support. Labor was weak and tended to have governmental support only during the two López P. administrations. With the end of the Liberal hegemony, the CTC (given its Liberal connections) was repressed by the government of Mariano Ospina. As a rival organization, the Union of Colombian Workers (UTC, Union de Trabajadores Colombianos) was founded by the Jesuits. The UTC was allowed to flourish during the Conservative years.

Both the UTC and the CTC supported the movement against Rojas Pinilla, although the former had grown rapidly during the Rojas dictatorship. Both were supporters of the National Front; however, it is safe to conclude that their power was considerably less than of the *gremios* during that period and now.

Two other labor federations exist today. One (the CSTC, Confederación Sindical de Trabajadores de Colombia) was formed in 1964 when numerous Communist-oriented unions banded together, after having been ejected from the CTC. The other (CGT, Confederación General de Trabajo), a socialist and radical-Christian labor federation, was formed in 1971. Both the CSTC and CGT existed without *personería jurídica* until it was granted by President López M. in 1974. There are still other labor unions at the enterprise level, but they remain unaffiliated with any of the four federations. Most recent estimates give the following breakdown of union membership: UTC, 40 percent; CTC, 25 percent; CSTC, 20-25 percent; other and unaffiliated, 10-15 percent.[15]

Several factors account for organized labor's weak position in Colombian politics. Labor leaders are still required to be full-time workers in their industries, a requirement that is enforced selectively. The division of labor into various federations has had obvious, detrimental effects to the movement. Perhaps two reasons are most important, however. One is that the percentage of the labor force that is unionized is small— only 17 to 19 percent in 1974, although the percentages were higher in industry, utilities, transportation, and communication. The other is that labor legislation has promoted the development of *enterprise* unions and weakened the possibilities of *industry-wide* unions. Further, strikes in manufacturing are limited legally to a maximum of forty days prior to the compulsory introduction of binding arbitration. This stipulation of the law, which has led some to conclude that Colombia has adopted many of the policies of the bureaucratic authoritarian regimes of the Southern Cone without the large-scale repression of them, weakens that key power resource of organized labor—the ability to paralyze the economy through strike actions.

The Rural and Urban Poor

The poor people of Colombia form a majority of the country and are also the least organized. To the extent that there has been organization, it has usually been directed by elite political leaders.

During the National Front, governments (along with various private agencies) put efforts into "community development" (Acción Comunal). This program had two major purposes: first, to contribute to the material well-being of poor people (primarily *campesinos*, but also urban dwellers) through community self-help projects such as schools and sewage systems, among many others; second, to alter the passivity of the Colombian *campesino* in the face of change. U.S. Peace Corps volunteers played an active role in this process. While this community-action program was supposed to develop juntas that would take the initiative at the local level, this seldom happened, and in many cases the programs collapsed when the *cuerpos de paz* left.

Another effort to organize the rural poor was through the UTC. An affiliate was formed (National Agrarian Association), which in the mid-1970s claimed to have 100,000 peasant members.

The most ambitious effort to organize the *campesinos* came, however, in 1967–1968 when President Lleras Restrepo attempted to develop a peasant counterweight to the large landowners. To this end, Lleras set up the National Association of Peasants (ANUC, Asociación Nacional de Usuarios Campesinos). By the end of the Lleras presidency in August 1970, almost 1 million peasants had been recruited to the organization.[16] By August 1971, ANUC (through its board of directors) had decided to divorce itself completely from all existing political parties and factions, because none was capable of responding to the demands of the peasantry. The board at the same time issued the "First Peasant Mandate," calling for expropriation of large landholdings without indemnification and free land distribution. This radicalization, as well as the ensuing land invasions, occupations of government buildings, boycotts, demonstrations, and other disruptive activities, brought ANUC into direct conflict with the government of Conservative President Pastrana. The response of the government was to divide, coopt, and repress. The more radical sector within ANUC (the majority one) was excluded from agrarian policymaking and repressed. The moderate wing, on the other hand, was given office space in the ministry of labor and other perquisites. This moderate wing, in atrophied state, still exists.

Today then, the *campesinos* are only slightly organized, while the urban poor (other than those in unionized jobs) are scarcely organized at all. Some of the latter do fall into Acción Comunal groups. The clear conclusion is that the poor in Colombia are numerically strong, but politically weak.

Guerrilla Groups

In recent years there have been four major guerrilla organizations in Colombia. They have been a constant nuisance to the government since the early 1960s, although it seems improbable that divided as they are (there are even reports of the different guerrilla groups fighting each other), they will be able to take power. Even if they were unified, a takeover seems unlikely—combined they probably number between 4,000 and 5,000 armed members.[17]

The first such group to emerge, towards the end of *La Violencia* in 1962, was the pro-Castro National Liberation Army (ELN, Ejército de Liberación Nacional). This was followed two years later by the Communist-dominated Revolutionary Armed Forces of Colombia (FARC, Fuerzas Armadas Revolucionarias Colombianas). For a few years after 1974 there was also a pro-Chinese People's Liberation Army (EPL, Ejército Popular de Liberación).

The best known of Colombian groups is the 19th of April Movement (M-19, Movimiento 19 de Abril), named after the date on which the election was "stolen" from Rojas Pinilla in 1970. M-19, claiming to be the armed branch of ANAPO, made its appearance in January 1974, when it stole a sword that belonged to Bolívar. The group was not considered a serious urban guerrilla threat until after it kidnapped and murdered the leader of the CTC in early 1976. M-19 also received international publicity when it tunneled into a Bogotá arsenal and stole arms (1979), when it kidnapped all those (including the U.S. ambassador) attending a cocktail party at the Dominican Republic embassy in Bogotá (1980), and when it kidnapped and executed a missionary from the United States (1981). While originally an urban guerrilla group, M-19 also participated in rural activities in Chocó and the Nariño-Putumayo areas in 1981.

The amount of popular support for the various guerrilla movements is open to speculation. It is alleged that the Colombian Communist party actively supports the FARC. Some student groups no doubt aid (and individual students join) the different movements. M-19 causes a reaction of amusement and admiration when it participates in such activities as distributing stolen food to the poor and robbing homes of the rich allegedly to give the take to the poor. However, it is impossible to state just how much popular support M-19 has. Some say that many would vote for the M-19 leader, Jaime Bateman, for president if he were allowed to run. He has not been allowed to.

The Turbay government, in 1981, pushed through congress an amnesty bill, in hopes that many of the *guerrilleros* would put down their arms. However, the amnesty was not unconditional and few took the opportunity.

The Armed Forces

After the dissolution of Gran Colombia in 1830, most of the Venezuelan officers who had come with Bolívar either left or were expelled from the country. The military was placed under an intellectual who reduced its size to under 2,500 men. They were controlled by the congress, that is, the civilian elite. Throughout the rest of the nineteenth century, the military as an institution was weak. The army played only a small role in the numerous civil wars, which were largely led by amateur officer-politicians from the two political parties.[18]

The first steps towards institutionalization came in the first decade of the twentieth century, following the disastrous War of the Thousand Days (1899–1902) and the loss of Panamá. President Rafael Reyes asked for a mission of the Chilean army, which responded positively. From this mission came the Escuela Militar, opened in 1907. Thus began the first formalized training of military officers. Yet the military remained small (proportionately the smallest in Latin America in 1932) and was slow to develop a sense of professionalism. Liberal-Conservative cleavages divided the officer corps, for example.

The military began growing in size with a border dispute with Peru in 1932–1933 and, more importantly, with World War II. The conclusion of that war found the Colombian military stronger and more united than ever before. By 1946 the military had stayed out of active politics for forty years. However, the Conservative governments during

La Violencia used the military for partisan purposes and, as a result of the system breakdown, in 1953 the military took over power.

Changes in the Military Role. In the early years of the National Front, the role of the military changed to one of primary responsibility for the planning and implementation of counterinsurgency, in this case, to end *La Violencia*. This change was reinforced when, in 1961, the policy of the U.S. government became one of military assistance programs geared to internal security. By 1962 the Colombian military, with U.S. assistance, was involved in developing antiguerrilla operations, intelligence techniques, and military civic-action programs. At the same time, the size of the military grew from 23,000 (1961) to 53,500 (1966). By 1980, it had reached 64,000.

Since these changes, there have been tensions about the role the military is to play: Should it remain apolitical, true to Colombian tradition? Or should it speak up about the social and economic problems of the nation? On at least three occasions (the first in 1965 and the last in 1981), individual military leaders have seen it necessary to talk about the basic problems of the society. In 1981 the commander of the army, General Landazábal Reyes, wrote in *Army Review*, "We are convinced that the army can militarily destroy the guerrillas, but we are also convinced that even with this, subversion will continue as long as the objective and subjective conditions in the economic, social, and political fields, which daily impair and disrupt stability, are not modified."[19] The first two military leaders who made similar statements were relieved of their posts; Landazábal, at this writing, is still a high military officer.

In the years since the end of the National Front, the role of the military has *increased* in Colombian politics. The resurgence of guerrilla activity in 1975 forced the military to increase counterinsurgency actions. But the most dramatic change came as a result of the Security Statute (Estatuto de Seguridad) of the Turbay government. Within a month after Turbay's inauguration, his minister of defense, General Camacho Leyva, announced an "unrestrained offensive" against guerrilla activities. With the Security Statute the military received power to try offenders. A vigorous campaign in 1979 led to the arrest of some 1,000 people, including artists and intellectuals, many of whom have stated that they were tortured. In 1980–1981 a "search and destroy" tactic was used in the El Pato–Guayabero region of Caquetá, displacing thousands of *campesinos*. In 1981, large numbers of troops were successful in defeating a M-19 invasion in southern Colombia.

Future of the Military. All of these happenings, and others, led to Colombian debates about the military during the Turbay years. On the one side were the people who argued that the military ruled, with civilians only as figureheads. General Camacho, they argued, was more powerful than President Turbay. The military, they said, had plans that even the civilian leaders did not know about. Human rights were being violated, as people were tortured and killed. Hundreds were held for long periods of time, without bail and without counsel, before being found innocent in courts martial. There had, in short, been an "Uruguayanization" of Colombian politics.

The other side argued that the military was doing no more or no less than what the elected civilians had instructed them to do. Camacho met almost daily with President Turbay, but the latter was the one making policy. Individual military men may use torture, but they are operating against orders when they do so.

Conclusions are difficult in this area, especially as military officers are typically less open with inquiring social scientists than civilian leaders are. Several tentative statements might be made, however.

First, to this point, the guerrillas in Colombia are not so serious a threat to the status quo as the *tupamaros* were in Uruguay. Further, the lower classes have not been mobilized so much as they were in Chile, by either political parties or labor unions. For these reasons, as well as historical tradition, a "bureaucratic authoritarian" regime seems unlikely at the moment. However, if the guerrillas were to become more powerful or the lower classes more mobilized in antiregime parties or labor unions, a greater role for the military might be probable.[20]

Second, under the Security Statute the military did have a more active role than at any time since at least 1958. In addition to being used in judicial and counterinsurgency activities, military forces have been used in campaigns in drug-producing areas of the country.

Third, it seems certain that there are at least some military officers who feel that the social and economic inequities of the society must be corrected. Their number is unknown, as well as their propensity to do more than speak and write about it.

Finally, apparently at this point the military still has not developed a corporate identity. Nor does it have prestige with civilians. Major interest groups would look with caution at a military regime and would actively oppose it if it had visions of a strong state, to the detriment of individual capitalism.

In short, a military coup would be received with mixed reactions in civilian life. In military circles, there would be great debate about what to do with power.

The Roman Catholic Church

The Colombian Roman Catholic church has long been considered one of the "strongest" in Latin America, although this "strength" has various aspects. As earlier chapters have shown, the church was *ad-*

Figure 4.1 Church and state in Colombia: the Plaza de Bolívar in Bogotá with (*left*) the National Cathedral and (*right*) the National Congress side by side.

ministratively strong during the colonial period; during the first years of independent history, it was *economically* strong, as a large landowner and controller of the *censos*. After the loss of economic power, the church remained *morally* strong, as most Colombians continued to be believers.

Yet the church hierarchy and the parish priests did favor one of the two political parties (the Conservatives), a position that must have weakened the church's strength with certain Liberals. This partisan position is seen in a 1949 statement of the National Bishops' Conference, in which the faithful were prohibited from voting for the Liberal candidates who might "wish to implant civil marriage, divorce, and co-education, which would open the doors to immorality and Communism."[21]

Another part of church strength came from its institutional relationship with the state. The Constitution of 1886, in its preamble, begins "In the name of God, Supreme source of all authority." The following year, a Concordat was signed between the government and the Vatican, defining the church's legal status and role. The church (as in the model of ideal Christendom of complete church-state integration) was described as an essential element of the social order and given a major role in various aspects of social life. Education at all levels was to be maintained in conformity with the dogma of the Catholic religion. The church was given the predominant role in registering births and the recording (and interring) of the dead. Marriage was placed under church control. Civil divorce did not exist; civil marriage for baptized Catholics was made contingent on a declaration of abandonment of the faith, to be made before a judge, posted publicly, and communicated to the local bishop. The church was also given broad civil powers for the more than 60 percent of the land designated as "mission territories."[22]

The Concordat was renegotiated in 1973, but few things were taken from the church's institutional power. There now is a possibility of civil divorce. Public statements are not necessary as before in order to have a civil marriage. But in other instances, the power of the church was increased. The missionary role was extended, with provisions made for a "special canonical regime" for mission territories and "marginal zones" (urban slum areas).

Yet change has come to the church in other ways. With urbanization came a loss of power of the Catholic church with the poor. Further, some priests began making the decision to support social and economic change. One notable example was Camilo Torres, educated both as a sociologist and a priest, who concluded that in Colombia in the mid-1960s to be a true Christian was to be a revolutionary. Camilo was defrocked, joined the ELN, and soon was killed in a skirmish with the army. In 1968, a group of "rebel priests" dedicated their efforts to changing the status quo.

Even at the top levels of the hierarchy, change has come, as can be seen in an analysis of the statements of the National Bishops' Conference of Colombia, which has been meeting since 1902. As early as the 1930s the hierarchy gradually began moving away from a predominant concern with the Liberal party and with socialism and began becoming more concerned with economic and social reform. *La Violencia* must have affected the bishops: how could one explain such a phenomenon in Catholic Colombia? By the 1950s, the bishops gradually withdrew from partisan involvement and began emphasizing national unity and an end to *La Violencia*. During the National Front, the hierarchy embraced the regime and supported Liberal presidents as well as Conservative ones.

Since the beginning of the National Front there has been a certain tension within the church hierarchy. On the one hand, the church is seen as a symbol of unity; on the other, there is the need for better distribution of wealth, and the conflict for it might cause disunity. This tension has led to a process of challenge and reevaluation within the hierarchy, and a certain eclecticism in the bishops' statements.

In 1969 in *The Church Facing Change*, the bishops expressed great concern for social problems, an acceptance of sociological analysis, and an openness to change. The bishops stressed the need for structural change in the economy and the society. They openly discussed poverty, unemployment, and economic dependency in a call for general political reforms to make further change possible. The negative features of

Colombian social life were discussed frankly, and, throughout, the call was for the bishops to look at social reality directly so as to prepare the clergy to deal with the social problems of the country.

Signs of caution and withdrawal began to appear almost immediately. In 1971, *Justice in the World* analyzed the Colombian situation in structural terms: poverty, unemployment, and social and political problems were directly addressed and explained as the result of unjust structures of power in the society. But when it came to action, the bishops were very cautious. Above all, they wanted to avoid breaking the "unity" of Colombian society, with the possible effect of violence. The church, they concluded, must stress unity over division and love over fear and hatred.

By 1976 (*Christian Identity in Actions for Justice*) the bishops had become so concerned with the possibility that an active church in the struggle for social change would divide the church that the conclusions were completely different from earlier ones. The Catholic Left and Liberation Theology (the growing number of priests who live with and aid the poor and quite often side with them against unjust leaders and economic structures) were bitterly criticized. It was argued that eschatological principles of the traditional Catholic faith could not be transformed into purely temporal ideas. As Daniel Levine points out, "They reject the transformation of the poor of the Gospels into the proletariat, the conversion of sin into social injustice, and the identification of evangelization with the promotion of social change and *concientización*. This transformation of religious concepts is seen as an attack on the very bases of the Catholic religion, removing its transcendental essence while undermining the recognized authority of the bishops—successors to the Apostles."[23] Liberation Theology was rejected for reasons both of policy and theology. As policy, Liberation Theology was deemed to be imprudent; as theology, to be wrong. This did not mean that the bishops were abandoning the search for social reform. Rather, they were rejecting the direct leadership of the church, which more properly would stimulate others to action. These others (capable lay people) would be guided by "authentic and authoritative" expositions of Catholic doctrine—that is to say, those provided by the bishops.

The bishops have remained active since 1976 and are likely to in the future. In late 1981 a statement by the bishops stated quite clearly that Colombian problems of insecurity of life, immorality, and crime were caused by the inequalities of the social system, which they termed "an inventory of abominations." There is, however, no indication that the Colombian church will become one dominated by Liberation Theology.

Yet the church hierarchy will continue to speak out when politicians raise the possibility of changes in areas considered to be church domain. Such happened during the presidential election of 1982, when candidate López suggested the possibility of easier divorce. The bishops replied,

> One who might not wish to commit treason to his faith cannot favor electoral platforms that include sharp blows to matrimony and to the family, that propose divorce in sacred matrimony, that intend to legalize the crime of abortion, that favor sterilization, that support antinatalist campaigns which include methods that contradict the teachings of the Church, that recommend materialist and lay education which closes the doors to the messages of the Faith. In the face of such proposals, and however much they might violate divine law, the Christian is obliged by conscience to abstain from favoring them with his vote.[24]

The U.S. Embassy

No discussion of groups in Colombia would be complete without some mention of one notable foreign actor, the U.S. government, as represented in its embassy in Bogotá and consulates in Medellín, Cali, and Barranquilla.

At times in recent years the embassy officials have played active roles in Colombian public policy. During the Alliance for Progress years, the Agency for International Development (AID) mission was important in policy decisions in a number of areas; agrarian reform, education, and population control were perhaps the most important. The Military Assistance Program has had effects in the Colombian military, and the embassy officials have played a role in Colombian policy in the drug field.

Perhaps today the U.S. government, as represented in the embassy, is less important than in the past. There is less foreign aid than before, and indeed the López M. government asked AID to leave the country. Perhaps this means a loss of "leverage," as the diplomats commonly call the influence that comes with the giving (or withdrawing) of foreign aid.

Yet there is too much in the historical record to completely discount the U.S. government as a pertinent "Colombian interest group." This will be discussed in Chapters 5 and 6.

CONCLUSIONS: THE DYNAMICS
OF GROUPS IN COLOMBIA

The above sections are straightforward and divided by topic. However, such an attempt at analysis (which by definition simplifies reality), especially one couched in a North American framework, misses at least four important characteristics of Colombian political behavior.

Government-institution Relationships

Colombia is not a perfect corporatist society, with the economic and social groups controlled by the political elite. But neither is it a pluralistic system in which groups are formed and operate with nearly complete freedom from government control. Rather, it is somewhere between these two ideal types. Some argue that although the government has the right to recognize legal groups (*personería jurídica*), this is a right seldom used. Yet I have shown above that two labor federations (CGT and CSTC) existed for some time before they were granted *personería jurídica*, and I discussed the repression of the radicals in ANUC by the Pastrana government. The safest conclusion is that *personería jurídica* is used selectively as a governmental tool in Colombia, rather than consistently as in other Latin American systems.

Further, the interrelationships of some interest groups and the government can be shown through citing the situation in the two most powerful *gremios*, the National Federation of Coffee Growers and the National Association of Industrialists. FEDECAFE has a national governing committee of eleven members. Of these, five are exofficio members—the ministers of foreign relations, economic development, finance, and agriculture and the government-appointed manager of the Agrarian Credit Bank. Further, the superintendent of banking (a governmental position) supervises the financial transactions of the federation; the president of the country appoints the manager of the federation from a list of three nominated by its national committee; and the manager acts as Colombia's official representative in international coffee negotiations. Still further, FEDECAFE has also "penetrated" the government. Its director sits on the board of directors of the Banco de la República and is a member of the CONPES.

In the case of ANDI, there are no governmental appointees on the governing board; however, ANDI has representatives on over a dozen governmental committees and boards of decentralized institutes at the national level, as well as even more representatives on lower-level and industrial committees.

Other groups have similar institutionalized connections with the government. Some even receive financial support from the national treasury. In short, this is not pluralism.

Family Relationships

In Colombian politics family relationships are extremely important, but complex. It is no doubt significant that, at one point in the late

1970s, brothers were at the same time president of the national senate and head of ANDI. This case is only one of many. Yet this is not to say that family members always agree. There also seems to be a willingness to overlook what a person is doing economically (and perhaps politically) if he or she is a family member. On one occasion I was interviewing a politician who was one of the leaders of the opposition to a coal contract with Exxon. During the interview, a nephew arrived, listened, and later gave his opinion. The politician stated, when his nephew had completed his statement, "Professor, you should realize that José works for Exxon. But that doesn't matter. He's a discreet person." I would hypothesize that this politician would never have said a similar thing about someone who was not a relative.

Roscas

This family relationship is extended beyond blood lines through the patronage-based *rosca*. In the government, belonging to the personalistic *rosca* of someone who obtains office is very important, and the higher the position received, the more important it is. No doubt thousands of individual careers depended on whether Galán, López, or Betancur won the 1982 presidential election. This extended not only to the ministries, but also to other jobs in the non-civil-service bureaucracy.

Further, *roscas* exist outside of politics in economic life. A very qualified bank official once told me that her resignation was expected when the man above her resigned his post. It was quite simple: the new head person might have a friend or relative whom he would appoint to her post. Perhaps this was best seen in a television commercial shown in Bogotá in 1980–1981, advertising a particular lottery that gave Renaults as the "fat prize." When the winner returned to his home driving the new car, his son asked, "Whose *rosca* did you get into?" This is not to suggest that personal connections and "old boy networks" are not also important in "modern" countries such as the United States; they surely are. The argument is simply that such personal contacts are more important in Colombia and are especially crucial given the centralization of power in the hands of a few people.

Informal Ties

As suggested by the preceding paragraphs, informal ties are no doubt more important than formal ones, including those formal overlapping memberships between economic interest groups and the government. Elite members in Colombia have much in common. They not only have the same social background, they also have gone to the same universities and, at times, belong to the same exclusive social clubs. Such personal ties are the subject of much lunchtime gossip in academic circles; to my knowledge, no one has ever tried to study them in a rigorous fashion.

NOTES

1. Confidential interview, former minister of mines and petroleum, May, 28, 1981.

2. Confidential interview, former minister of economic development, April 10, 1981.

3. Confidential interview, former minister of *hacienda*, April 20, 1981.

4. Miguel Urrutia, "Diversidad ideológica e integración Andina," *Coyuntura Económica*, 10, 2 (1980): 197.

5. Confidential interview, former minister of *hacienda*, April 20, 1981.

6. The information for this section on planning in Colombia comes from Angel Israel Rivera Ortiz, "The Politics of Development Planning in Colombia," Ph.D. dissertation, State University of New York at Buffalo, 1976, pp. 65, 67, 71, 76, 77, 104.

7. *Latin America Weekly Report* (London), November 13, 1981.

8. Orlando Fals Borda, *Subversión y Cambio Social* (Bogotá: Ediciones Tercer Mundo, 1968), p. 117.

9. Statement at the Universidad de los Andes, Bogotá, 1981.

10. Luis Carlos Galán, "El nuevo liberalismo," *El Tiempo,* June 8, 1981, p. 5-A.

11. Gary Hoskin, "The Colombian Political Party System: Electoral Domination and System Instability," Paper given at the U.S. State Department Conference on Colombia, November 9, 1981, p. 31.

12. The information for this section comes from Jonathan Hartlyn, "Interest Groups and Political Conflict in Colombia: A Retrospective and Prospective View," Paper given at the U.S. State Department Conference on Colombia, November 9, 1981.

13. This point was brought to my attention by Jonathan Hartlyn, in his reactions to the first draft of this chapter.

14. *Latin America Weekly Report* (London), January 8, 1982.

15. Hartlyn, Table 4.

16. Information for this section comes from Bruce Michael Bagley, "Political Power, Public Policy and the State in Colombia: Case Studies of the Urban and Agrarian Reforms during the National Front, 1958–1974" Ph.D. dissertation, University of California, Los Angeles, 1979; and "Beyond the National Front: State and Society in Contemporary Colombia," Paper given at the U.S. State Department Conference on Colombia, November 9, 1981.

17. Information in this section and the following one comes from Daniel L. Premo, "The Armed Forces and Colombian Politics: In Search of a Mission," mimeographed (Chestertown, Md.: Washington College, 1981).

18. J. Mark Ruhl, *Colombia: Armed Forces and Society*, Foreign and Comparative Studies, Latin American Series (Syracuse, N.Y.: 1980), p. 18.

19. Quoted in Premo, p. 31.

20. J. Mark Ruhl, "An Alternative to the Bureaucratic-Authoritarian Regime: The Case of Colombian Modernization," *Inter-American Economic Affairs* 35, 2 (1981) suggests that the lack of populist parties in Colombia is one of the major reasons that there has been no bureaucratic authoritarianism.

21. John D. Martz, *Colombia: A Contemporary Political Survey* (Chapel Hill: University of North Carolina Press, 1962), p. 84.

22. This analysis is based on the excellent analysis in Daniel H. Levine, *Religion and Politics in Latin America: The Catholic Church in Venezuela and Colombia* (Princeton: Princeton University Press, 1981), especially pp. 70–96.

23. Ibid., pp. 92–93.

24. *El Espectador* (Bogotá), March 14, 1982.

5

The Colombian
Mixed Economy
and Public Policies

This chapter describes the Colombian economy as it exists today, with a historical analysis of various stages of its evolution within "dependency," and considers the major public policies of recent presidents. Although it is certain that some of the public policies are not *directly* economic in scope, almost all have indirect economic consequences.

OVERVIEW: THE COLOMBIAN ECONOMY TODAY

When one thinks of the Colombian economy, coffee usually first comes to mind. This is a correct first impression in one sense, but a misleading one in another. Coffee is the leading *legal* export, and investment in capital goods, which are usually imported, historically has been highly dependent on coffee earnings. However, coffee production makes up only about 4 percent of the gross domestic product (GDP), and growth of the country's GDP is not highly dependent on coffee earnings, at least in the short run.[1]

The economy today is still predominantly a primary-sector one. This sector (agriculture, fishing, and mining) makes up 28 percent of the GDP, down from 39 percent in 1950–1951. The manufacturing sector is 21 percent of the GDP, up from 17 percent in 1950–1951. Other economic activities include commerce (18 percent), services (12 percent), and transportation (5 percent). A "miscellaneous" category makes up the final 16 percent.[2] Many of these changes resulted from explicit governmental policies; others were caused by exogenous factors.

A recent development is the importance of the "other economy" based on illegal trade. While contraband is an old Colombian tradition in border regions, the 1970s showed an order-of-magnitude increase, primarily through the growth of an illicit drug trade.

Colombia's economic performance has been satisfactory, but not spectacular, since World War II. Annual growth of GDP averaged 5.1 percent during the 1960s (below the average of 6.1 percent for "middle income" developing countries) and 6.0 percent from 1970 to 1979 (above the 5.5 percent average for those countries). At no time was there a long period of slowdowns; most of them lasted no more than one year. Then in 1979 the growth rate declined to 5.1 percent and to between 3 and 4 percent in the following year.[3]

Coffee is still the leading legal export, although "minor" exports have become more important since 1967 (see Table 5.1). Trade with the United States is especially important (22 percent of all exports and 34 percent of all imports in 1977), although a great deal less so than thirty years ago. Coffee's percentage of legal export earnings fell until the coffee "boom" of the late 1970s; the percentage of coffee going to the United States has fallen to about 30 percent (1979), with West Germany occupying a close second position (26 percent). Imports are predominantly raw materials and intermediate goods (52 percent in 1980), followed by capital goods (35 percent) and consumer goods (12 percent).[4] In short, while Colombia is still a dependent country, it is no longer a country that trades predominantly in one product with one advanced industrial country.

The economy does not fit neatly into a category of "capitalist" or "socialist," or even "state capitalist." The key characteristic is that it is a mixed economy. The state is considered to have a primary role in leading the nation out of underdevelopment. It owns most infrastructure (roads, railroads, and telecommunications) and other costly, but important, activities (electricity). It is expected that the state will develop energy resources (but in what fashion is another question, as will be shown below) since, with some few exceptions, subsoil rights are the patrimony of the state. At times, the state is expected to begin industry that is considered essential for national development, when private investment will not do so. However, once these industries are on a profit-making basis, the state typically sells them to private enterprise (as was the case with the Paz del Rio steel mill).

In short, the Colombian state is supposed to supply (at least for a time) those things that the country needs, but that private industrialists either cannot or will not invest in. The tradition, going back to the Spanish colony, was even stronger in the nineteenth century. However,

Figure 5.1 Coffee growing: *above*, picking beans; *below*, the traditional method of transporting them by mule.

Table 5.1

Characteristics of Colombian Foreign Trade, 1970-1979

Year	Legal Exports (Millions US$)	Percent Coffee	Total Imports (Millions US$)	"Other Economy" (Millions US$)
1970	643	59	598	
1971	656	52	652	
1972	841	49	702	
1973	1,009	48	760	
1974	1,214	41	1,117	
1975	1,414	44	1,403	
1976	1,652	51	1,312	
1977	2,243	61	1,843	
1978	2,569	66	2,188	
1979	3,410	59	3,031	3,200

Sources: Legal exports and total imports, 1970-1978, "Analisis del sector externo colombiano," Revista ANDI, 48 (1980), p. 54; Percent coffee, 1970-1978, ibid., p. 55; Legal exports, total imports, and percent coffee, 1979, División de Estudios Económicos, DANE, "El Comercio exterior colombiano en 1979," Revista Mensual de Estadística, 348 (1980), p. 34; "Other economy," Richard B. Craig, "Domestic Implications of Illicit Drug Cultivation, Processing and Trafficking in Colombia," Paper delivered at the U.S. State Department Conference on Colombia, November 9, 1981, p. 4.

the growth of private capitalism—especially at the beginning in the Medellín area—led to a state role in the economy that is probably among the weakest in Latin America. It is generally assumed that the state cannot operate things as efficiently as the private sector can (at least the state as it exists now), and there is little indication of a "state ideology" among the higher levels of the state itself.

Yet the state's involvement, through taxation, tariff and exchange rates, and policy toward other countries and multinational corporations, is extremely important to the economy. Also important are factors exogenous to Colombia, including the weather in Brazil, for example. One important theme of this chapter is that the combination of politicians' decisions and exogenous factors have led to the Colombian economy today.

HISTORICAL DEVELOPMENT OF THE ECONOMY

The Colombian economy has always existed in a condition of *economic dependency,* a term that has been used increasingly in the last two decades, albeit with varying definitions. By this term I mean that historically the economy has been one that responds more to economic conditions *outside* of the country than to those inside it. The relevant external factors have been the developed economies of the world— particularly European countries in the nineteenth century, the United States between 1900 and 1969 (the dates being a bit arbitrary), and the United States, Japan, and the European Economic Community countries since 1970.

Using the concept of dependency, the Colombian economy can be classified into four time periods: classic dependency with no stable export crop (1830–1880); classic dependency with a stable export crop (1880–1930); dependent development with emphasis on import substitution (1930–1967); and dependent development with emphasis on export diversification (1967 to the present). The first three periods are considered in this section.

Classic dependency was the exchange of Colombian primary products for foreign manufactured goods. The first period (1830–1880) was an unstable one, simply because there was no stable Colombian product that could be exported in foreign trade. Fluctuations in quantity and value of exports of gold, quinine, tobacco, and other products gave the country hard currencies with which to buy manufactured goods, primarily from Great Britain. While in part this can be explained by the prior establishment and economies of scale of British industries, the Colombian leaders saw this as a desirable path for the country to take (even if it did do harm to some native artisan industry). The period was one of nineteenth-century economic liberalism, and within Colombia the Liberal party was in power for most of the time. An explicit statement of this division of labor was made in 1847 by treasury secretary Florentino González:

In a country rich in mines and agricultural products, which can sustain a considerable and beneficial export trade, the law should not attempt to encourage industries that distract the inhabitants from the agricultural and mining occupations. . . . Europe with an intelligent population, and with the possession of steam power and its applications, educated in the art of manufacturing, fulfills its mission in the industrial world by giving various forms to raw materials. We too should fulfill our mission, and there is no doubt as to what it is, if we consider the profusion of natural resources with which Providence has endowed this land. We should offer Europe raw materials and open our doors to her manufactures, to facilitate trade and the profit it brings, and to provide the consumer, at a reasonable price, with the products of the manufacturing industry.[5]

The second period (roughly 1880 to 1930) was different from the first in that coffee represented a stable export crop; earnings from coffee exports could be used for manufactured imports. By 1878 coffee earnings represented 13.5 percent of total exports, and the percentages increased rapidly after that, reaching a high of 80 percent in 1924.[6] With this situation came increasing dependence on the United States (added to by other geophysical realities at the turn of the century). While earlier products had been traded with a variety of nations, coffee went predominantly to the colossus of the north, particularly after World War I. Imports were less concentrated than exports, but here again the majority came from the United States.

Even during the second period, import-substitution industrialization (ISI) began. Some manufacturing (especially in consumer nondurables) began as early as the first decade of this century, and ISI increased during the trade cutoff during World War I. It was, however, the years of the Great Depression that saw a quantum leap in ISI. Yet this "dependent development" did not indicate an end to dependency. Rather, foreign trade became more important than ever, as industrialization had been achieved using imported capital goods and the replacement parts for them. Dependency in the third period, therefore, consisted of exporting coffee in order to buy capital goods. Coffee exports were encouraged as much as, if not more than, before.

Colombian leaders realized the difficulties with such a one-crop export. Other products were exported, some through multinational corporation enclaves (bananas on the Caribbean coast; petroleum—which became the second largest "traditional" export; gold, with MNCs increasingly purchasing Colombian mines). But in 1964, for example, coffee made up 79 percent of export earnings. The problem was obvious: world coffee prices fluctuated according to supply and demand (particularly the former). When "acts of God," such as a frost in Brazil, led to temporary shortages in world supply and hence higher prices, Colombian export earnings (and therefore ability to import) boomed. When world supply normalized—and when the new nations of Africa entered into the market—prices plummeted, and so did the ability to import.

PUBLIC POLICY SINCE 1958

Perhaps all Colombian politicians since 1958, and maybe even before, have agreed that there should be "economic development." However, there have been recurrent debates about just what economic development is and about how best to obtain it if an agreed-upon definition is reached.

The first question centers around whether or not development is more than economic growth. In the early 1980s, *Estrategia económica y financiera*, a leading Bogotá economic journal, stated that Colombia could be a developed country in twenty years. When I asked one of the writers for the journal just what was meant by this, he replied, "We mean that Colombia will have a gross domestic product per capita equal to that of Spain—or even Italy—today."[7] Other Colombians, many of whom are radicals, argue that true economic development comes only with diversification of the economy and/or less dependency on foreign capital, technology, and know-how. Some of these people also consider *redistribution* of wealth to be as important as mere economic growth, if not more so.

Historical analysis shows that the people in power have usually defined development in the first way above—economic growth. However, they then debate the best way to achieve such growth. Should coffee be emphasized as Colombia's natural "comparative advantage," or should growth come through import substitution and/or more diversified exports? What is the role of the manufacturing sector to be? What about the value of the peso: should a high rate of exchange be maintained so as to encourage exports or a low rate to encourage imports? What priority does the control of inflation have? The questions could be continued; the point is that well-trained (quite often in the United States) economists, engineers, and politicians who make up the Colombian elite disagree on how best to accomplish economic growth.

Almost all research on Colombian public policy agrees that the president is the key person. If an individual as president is not willing or able to use his power to bring about coordination—through threats, promises, and just the incredibly tiring work of persuasion—there surely will be none. Even if the president is willing and able to coordinate, the vested interests of the economic interest groups—both Colombian and multinational—might prevent the best-prepared and most able president from implementing public policies, especially redistributive ones. It is appropriate to consider public policy in chronological order, by presidency, even though one must be careful in distinguishing between what the presidents *say* they are going to do (through their development plans published early in their terms) and what they actually are *able* to do.

The First Half of the National Front:
Lleras Camargo and Valencia

The first two National Front presidents had as their main priority the reestablishment of peace in the countryside. This policy was largely successful. The same could not be said about other public policies.

During the presidency of Alberto Lleras Camargo, there were policies of tax reform (although not really implemented until 1967, at the earliest) and of public school expansion. Perhaps, however, the most notable policy was that of agrarian reform. Law 135 of 1961 set forth six propositions to correct the overconcentration of land resources. They were designed to:

1. eliminate and prevent the inequitable concentration of land or its subdivision into uneconomic units; reconstitute adequate units of cultivation in the *minifundio* zones; provide lands to those who lacked them
2. promote adequate economic use of unused and deficiently used lands, by means of programs designed to secure their well-balanced distribution and rational utilization
3. increase farm productivity by the application of appropriate techniques; endeavor to have land used in the way best suited to its location and characteristics
4. give small tenants and sharecroppers greater guarantees of security of tenure and make it easier for them and for wage laborers to gain ownership of land
5. elevate the level of living of the rural population, through the measures already indicated, and through the coordination and promotion of services for technical assistance, agricultural credit, housing, marketing, health and social security, storage and preservation of products, and the promotion of cooperatives
6. insure the conservation, defense, improvement, and adequate utilization of natural resources.

To implement Law 135, a Colombian Agrarian Reform Institute (IN-CORA, Instituto Colombiano de la Reforma Agraria) was created, staffed originally with young lawyers, economists, and sociologists who were seriously interested in changing the land tenure structure.[8] This land reform a few years later was supported (and in part financed) through the Alliance for Progress. The role played by the Agency for International Development is discussed in Chapter 6.

This agrarian reform, almost all students agree, was largely a failure. The original proposal, drafted by Carlos Lleras Restrepo, went much farther. It was watered down during congressional consideration and never effectively implemented. Although land titles were given to 54,000 families between 1961 and 1967, there were somewhere between 400,000 and 500,000 landless families. The total land distributed was 4,275,000 hectares (10,556,000 acres); of this, the highest percentage came from colonization of public lands (46 percent). Only about 1 percent of the total came from expropriations.[9]

The presidency of Conservative Guillermo León Valencia (1962–1966) did see the end of La Violencia and, for that matter, the beginning of leftist guerrilla bands in the mountains. Valencia continued many of the Lleras Camargo policies, although it must be admitted candidly that he lacked the inclination or ability to coordinate the disparate governmental and economic interests in order to make policy. Valencia's presidency is remembered as an ineffectual one, with one notable faux pas—the chief executive's toasting Spain rather than France during a state visit of Charles DeGaulle!

The Carlos Lleras Restrepo Presidency

By the time of the inauguration of Carlos Lleras Restrepo (1966), the economy had suffered from almost a decade of low coffee prices and the resultant trade deficits, the Lleras Camargo land reform had obviously failed, and there had been little public policy for at least four years. The new president was a trained economist, with definite ideas of how things should be changed and with the ability to coordinate the government. Policy changes during his presidency came through four initiatives: (1) Decree-Law 444, (2) another agrarian reform, (3) the first Colombian population policy, and (4) the creation of the Andean Pact (to be considered in Chapter 6).

Decree-Law 444. Enacted in 1967, Decree-Law 444 had three major parts. One encouraged "minor" exports more than ever. Some students go so far as to see this law as the beginning of a fourth period of Colombian economic history: the period of dependent development with emphasis on export diversification. Diversified exports were to become the "motor" for development, rather than either coffee exports or ISI (which had reached limits in Colombia later to be seen in other Latin American countries, due to the lack of the growth of intermediate-goods and capital-goods sectors).

The law decreed a simple and general tax credit for the exporters of "minor" products (that is, all except coffee and petroleum). A general

Figure 5.2 Former President Carlos Lleras Restrepo (1966–1970)

tax-credit certificate (CAT, *certificado de abono tributario*), originally set at 15 percent of the export value, was given to minor exporters. It could be used in payment of taxes one year after the date of issue. The CATs were freely negotiable. Law 444 also set up an Export Promotion Fund (PROEXPO), a decentralized institute that channels credit under liberal terms to exporting firms, provides equity capital under special circumstances, insures against political and noncommercial export risks, helps prepare export plans, tries to promote an "export mentality" in Colombia, and advertises and holds trade fairs abroad.[10] While minor exports had been encouraged by earlier laws, Decree-Law 444 had a much greater effect. These exports grew rapidly (15 percent in the first two years alone) and by 1974 had become more important than coffee (petroleum no longer was being exported). These minor exports (especially bananas, cotton, sugar, and tobacco, but also gold, paper and cardboard, meat, wood, shoes, seafood, glass, oilseed cakes, chemicals, furs, cement, hides, precious stones, tires, books, fresh-cut flowers, and dog toys[11]) provided foreign exchange to purchase consumer, capital, and intermediate goods. Although dependency had not been left behind, the monoculture seemed to have been, until July 1974, when there was a major frost in Brazil, the effects of which are discussed below.

The adoption of Decree-Law 444 did not mean that coffee was neglected. Every Colombian government since 1967 has been supportive of coffee production and exportation, and a close relationship exists between governments and the National Federation of Coffee Growers. Minor exports were to be *in addition to* coffee, not instead of it. Neither was import substitution industrialization discouraged. It simply was not the *major* goal as in previous governments.

A second part of Decree-Law 444 regulated multinational corporations for the first time, leaving behind a period that could be called laissez faire in the Colombian state's dealings with them. Article I of the law stated that foreign private investment would have to be in harmony with the national interest. Any private investment greater than US$100,000 would have to be approved by the government. A complex institutional machinery was set up to enforce the stipulations. The National Planning Department (DNP) analyzes and approves investment proposals. The Exchange Office (Oficina de Cambios) registers and authorizes the outflow of capital. The Superintendent of Foreign Commerce (the director of INCOMEX) grants import licenses. The Advisory Committee on Global Licenses (Comité Asesor de Licencias Globales) is in charge of implementing the government policies on capital-goods imports and of avoiding excess unused productive capacity.[12] In so doing, the Lleras government hoped to have accurate data on MNC investment for the first time, to control repatriation of profits (a limit of 14 percent of investment was set), and to make certain that MNCs would not force Colombian enterprises out of business.

Through this law, President Lleras and his advisers were reacting to a very real problem. MNC investment in Colombia, especially that from the United States after World War I, had sizable interests in high-technology and service fields. By the end of 1966, total investment by MNCs was US$466 million, particularly in the fields of chemicals, pharmaceuticals, food, tires, and electrical machinery.[13] While MNC investment was not as great as in Mexico or Brazil, some Colombians considered it very significant.

A third element of Decree-Law 444 was the establishment of a "crawling peg" exchange rate. Previously, a set exchange rate had led to balance-of-payments crises and to large devaluations. After Decree-Law 444 there were continuing small devaluations, coming from "free market" transactions. In theory, these devaluations would keep up with inflation; by and large this was true until the mid-1970s.

The Lleras Restrepo Agrarian Reform. Since it was apparent that the Lleras Camargo agrarian reform (written by Lleras Restrepo) had largely failed, there was a new attempt. The basic goal of Law 1 of 1968 was to accelerate the pace of land distribution by eliminating the legal and financial restrictions that had slowed or prevented the application of provisions of Law 135 of 1961. The new law also intended to increase overall levels of production in the commercial agricultural sector by reorganizing state credit mechanisms, increasing the total amount of resources available for agriculture, and providing tax incentives for exporting nontraditional agricultural products (that is, other than coffee and cattle).[14]

This law had a redistributive orientation—as indeed Carlos Lleras himself had long had—and some redistributive effects. INCORA's activities increased, with over one-half of all negotiated purchases and almost two-thirds of all expropriations of the period 1961–1971 taking place in the last two years of the period. Nevertheless, even by the end of the Lleras presidency, the overall impact of the agrarian reform program on the country's land tenure system was still extremely limited.

Population Policy. Despite the fact that the 1964 census showed that the Colombian population had grown by 3 percent annually since 1951, no government before Lleras Restrepo had a policy about this extremely important issue. In large part this was no doubt due to the power of the church. Indeed, this can be seen quite clearly: After Alberto Lleras, in August 1965, stated as a private citizen at an international meeting that the government should undertake action favoring smaller families and slower population growth, he was criticized by the church hierarchy.[15]

During the Carlos Lleras presidency, the government did state such a policy publicly, and the president was the only one from Latin America to sign the Declaration on Population of the United Nations (UN). In the same year (1966) the ministry of health signed a contract for a program of training and research that included family planning in addition to maternal and child health.

The results of this policy—only making family planning available— were impressive. In 1967 about 35,000 women participated in family-planning services in one of the private clinics supported by foreign donors (AID, the Rockefeller and Ford foundations, and international agencies based in Sweden and Canada). That number had grown to 164,000 by 1972, and a survey conducted in mid-1973 in Bogotá indicated that about one-half of the women were using some form of contraception.

This public policy issue contrasts in many ways with others considered in this chapter. In the first place, much of the impetus came from foreign sources, who between 1965 and 1972 donated a total close to US$15 million. In the second place, the church was the only organized group that opposed the policy. Other groups, including both medical personnel and planners (the first because they realized the human cost of rapid population growth, the second because they understood the economic costs), supported the policy.[16]

The result was the most thorough antinatalist policy in any Latin

American country. It is certain that other factors led to decreased fertility, most notably urbanization. With the benefit of data now available, we can see that population growth was declining even before the Lleras policy. However, few would argue that family-planning clinics had no effect on the change.

The Pastrana Government

The Pastrana government (1970–1974) continued many of the Lleras R. policies, such as those on population, the Andean Pact, the promotion of minor exports, and a more progressive fiscal policy. In two cases—agrarian reform and construction—there were, however, notable differences.

The Pastrana economic policy was centered on the "leading sector" concept, that is, the choice of one sector—one with "multiplier" effects on the rest of the economy—that would be emphasized. The sector chosen was construction, particularly in the cities. It was argued that many unskilled people could be put to work in that sector, and when they spent their earnings, the multiplier effect would benefit much of the rest of the country. Further, this strategy had the advantage that it could be done with few imports.

Much government investment went into the "leading sector." The way to encourage private investment was the introduction of the Unidades de Poder Adquisitivo Constante (UPAC, a constant-value investment in which one's deposit is increased not only with interest but also with an inflation factor). Since the investments were corrected for inflation, so too were the mortgages. Soon many things in Colombian society were "upaquizado" ("UPACed"): life insurance benefits (and premiums) and, much less formally, wages and prices. Soon the UPAC concept— and the overheating of the economy with massive investment in construction—led to a general inflation mentality. Inflation reached a high of 27 percent in 1974.

Also during the Pastrana years there was one last attempt at agrarian reform. After his narrow victory over Rojas Pinilla, Pastrana promised redistributive reforms in a number of areas. The land-reform proposal, however, contained several aspects that were very threatening to the large agriculture groups. Most important was the renta presuntiva (presumed income) that would tax the estimated income of agricultural land, based on a complex formula taking into account such factors as region, type of crops or livestock, soil qualities, and climatic conditions.[17] This stipulation led to much controversy and a bargaining process among the different factions of the political parties and the different agricultural groups that led to an agreement in which the government made major concessions to large landowners on questions of productivity levels and land taxes. This agreement also guaranteed large infusions of new credit into the sector for *modern* (which is to say, capital-intensive) agricultural development. The agreement also had a highly modified form of the *renta presuntiva*.

It was not surprising that little land redistribution came from the final Pastrana laws after that agreement. Indeed, one expert has termed these laws as "the counterreform," meaning quite simply that agricultural *production* had become more important than redistribution of lands.[18] None of the redistributive laws were very effective. Organized groups were able to block and water down laws; enforcement was difficult because of the lack of trained personnel and because landowners could tie up the reform in lengthy litigation. Further, even AID officials (after it became evident that there would not be Castros in other countries) waffled between redistribution and increased production, finally stressing the latter by the mid-1960s.

The López Michelsen Government

When Alfonso López Michelsen was inaugurated as president on August 7, 1974, there was a certain amount of optimism. The National Front had ended, and López had received a large majority in the presidential election. Further, López was considered by many to be a "progressive" Liberal: he had, after all, been the leader of the MRL during part of the National Front. Further, in his public pronouncements (and in his four-year plan, called "To Close the Gap") López called for a much more explicit attack on poverty and inequality, more concern with efficiency, and control of inflation. The central theme of the plan was "to close the gaps that the traditional model of development has created . . . to reduce the gaps between country and city, the gap between rich and poor barrios, the gap between those who have access to health services and education and the illiterate and undernourished."[19]

The López government soon declared an "economic emergency," which gave it the ability to rule by decree power. An economic team had been working in secret since late May, making plans for the first months. This allowed the government to make many economic changes in a ninety-day period, most notably a tax reform.

This tax reform covered the sales tax, export taxes and incentives, adjustments of tariffs on imports, tax treatment of government agencies, and personal and company income taxes. In general, the goals of the tax reform were to: (1) increase the progressivity of the tax system, (2) reduce distortions of the tax system on the allocation of resources, (3) promote economic stability by increasing revenue and by enhancing the built-in response of the tax system to growth in national income, and (4) simplify the administration and compliance of the tax system and hence to reduce evasion and increase yields.[20]

In 1975 three phenomena came together (all of which had begun before the López presidency), causing public policy to shift to inflation control. These were the new status of Colombia as a petroleum importer (at a time when the Organization of Petroleum Exporting Countries [OPEC] had increased international prices threefold), the massive amount of foreign currencies coming into the country through illicit drug trade, and the coffee "bonanza" following the July 1974 frost in Brazil. All three of these occurrences put inflationary pressure on the López government, and in so doing made monetary control the key policy of the administration. Government investments "to close the gap" had to be delayed, or indeed cancelled.

The Energy Question. Petroleum development began in Colombia in 1921 with the entrance of the first U.S. petroleum company (Tropical, a subsidiary of Standard of New Jersey). Gulf followed a few years later, and as the decades went on, more MNCs arrived. The typical contract was a "concession" one, in which the MNC had complete control of the operation, both production and refining, and for which the government received certain taxes and royalties. By 1950, 412 million barrels of Colombian crude had been exported by the MNCs, especially to the United States.[21] In the 1960s, the government was receiving only about US$0.25 per barrel.

In 1951 the first Tropical contract ended, and the area that the MNC had exploited for thirty years (the so-called Concesión De Mares) reverted to the Colombian government, as did the refinery at Barrancabermeja, the largest in the country. To continue exploitation of the area, after Colombian capitalists were offered it and refused, the government of Laureano Gómez founded the Colombian Petroleum Enterprise (ECOPETROL). ECOPETROL soon discovered that the most accessible petroleum had already been taken (although far from all, as the Concesión De Mares region is still in production today), and that they had a refinery that they could not run. They therefore contracted with Tropical to run the refinery an additional ten years, during which time Colombian technicians were trained.[22]

During the Rojas Pinilla years, Cities Services offered an alternative contract to the concession model. This was the "association" contract, a kind of joint-venture contract. In this model the MNC does the exploration at its own risk and cost. If an economically feasible amount of petroleum is found, the MNC and the government invest equally in production activities. The government receives royalties from the MNC, as well as other taxes, and 50 percent of the petroleum. Actual production is run by the MNC (as "operator") and the entire enterprise is governed

Figure 5.3 Part of the ECOPETROL refinery, Barrancabermeja

by an executive committee, composed of one representative of the MNC and one of ECOPETROL, which makes all major decisions by majority vote.

By the time that López Michelsen was inaugurated, there had been over a decade of debate about petroleum production. It was clear that Colombian consumption was increasing (it had reached 48.5 million barrels in 1973), whereas production was stable before 1970 and declining thereafter. Therefore exports (including those of ECOPETROL after 1951) were down to fewer than 10 million barrels a year. (A total of over 1 billion barrels of crude had been exported by that time, with the highest point coming in 1965 when 40 million were exported.)[23] During those debates, one side (the MNCs and the Colombians who agreed with them) argued that the foreign companies were doing their best and could do even better if incentives for exploration were increased. The other side (including one minister of mines who, in effect, was forced out of office by the MNCs) argued that the MNCs had found ample crude, but were only waiting until the government gave them better prices.

Whichever side was right, López found his country in a position of the second leading export—petroleum—now being an import. His government replied by decreeing that all future petroleum contracts would be association ones (not ending the concessions that were in force, however) and by stating that all "new" crude and all that obtained by "enhanced" recovery methods would be bought at OPEC prices, CIF Cartagena. Exploration in the following years did increase, and by the early 1980s production increased for the first time in a decade. Some politicians were content. The association contract, they stated, was a more nationalistic one than the concession. Others argued that, while such was correct, the association just did not go far enough. They insisted that the Colombian government was never an equal in such contracts; rather, it played the role of "horse" while the MNC was the "jockey," making all the decisions.[24]

A related question was that of coal development, which also came to a head during the López years. There are records indicating that the Indians were using the mineral at the time of the arrival of the Spanish. In the first century of independence, coal production was begun by Colombians, and by 1974 the annual production was in the neighborhood of 3.5 million metric tonnes (3.86 million short tons). Almost all coal production was owned by Colombians; the great majority of production was in small mining *minifundios*, although there is some evidence that Nicaraguan dictator Anastasio Somoza Debayle ("Tachito") had some stock in one of the large companies.

The most promising Colombian coal deposit (of the many spread all over the country) was that of the La Guajira peninsula called El Cerrejón, discovered in 1872 by a foreigner. Until 1982 there was no production. In the 1950s the Industrial Promotion Institute (IFI) began a series of studies of the area (although Tropical had done some in 1946). In 1969, IFI founded a commercial enterprise (Cerrejón Carboneras) to arrange for the exploitation of the area, and in 1972 a "memorandum of agreement" was signed with Peabody Coal, a subsidiary of Kennecott Copper, for the Central Cerrejón area.

The history that followed, in the late Pastrana and early López administrations, is rather complex and somewhat cryptic.[25] In June 1974 International Colombia Resources Corporation (INTERCOR), a Canadian subsidiary of Exxon, produced a draft contract for the North and South Cerrejón areas. INTERCOR proposed an association contract, much like those used already in petroleum. This contract was never signed because either the Pastrana government or Exxon refused.

In October 1975 both IFI and ECOPETROL asked the ministry of mines for the right to develop the north and south areas. ECOPETROL received that right and in the same month sent a model contract out to bid to seventeen MNCs. The model contract was one of association. In February 1976 proposals were received from six MNCs. In the same month, the minister of mines announced that an impasse had been reached with Peabody for the central zone and that the MNC was withdrawing from the country.

In November 1976 the Colombian Coal Company (CARBOCOL, Carbones de Colombia) was established as a "second-level" state enterprise. That level indicated that all the stock was owned by other, "first-level" state enterprises, including IFI and ECOPETROL. In December 1976 CARBOCOL signed a contract with INTERCOR (now a U.S. subsidiary of Exxon) for the North Cerrejón area, as that MNC offered the highest royalties (15 percent).

In June 1977 CARBOCOL began working in the central area in "a direct and independent" form. The major debates about coal policy, during the Turbay administration, are discussed below.

Drug Trade. Colombia's role in the international drug market developed very rapidly. It is estimated that, although in 1970 the country exported relatively small amounts of cocaine and marijuana, by 1979 it shipped some 37 metric tonnes (40.8 short tons) of cocaine and 15,000 tonnes (16,538 short tons) of marijuana. The Sierra Nevada region in Caribbean coastal Colombia, including parts of the *departamentos* of Guajira, Cesar, and Magdalena, became the world's largest area of marijuana cultivation after the 1975 herbicide spraying in Mexico. This area had, by 1978, 19,000 hectares (46,914 acres) of marijuana cultivation, employing some 18,500 people.

Estimates of the exact amounts of cultivation—and foreign earnings—are guesses at best. One study concluded that the total earnings of the "other economy" in 1979 were US$3.2 billion, and one might make similar estimates for the López years. Of this total, US$2.15 billion (about 70 percent) came from marijuana; US$460 million (11 percent) from cocaine; and the remaining 11 percent from "traditional" contraband in coffee (US$150 million), sugar, cattle, and cement (US$440 million).[26] Not unlike other parts of the Colombian economy, the small marijuana farmer receives only about 7 percent of the total export value; the high concentrations of income from marijuana and cocaine are in the hands of a few people. Summarizing his conclusions, one North American scholar has recently stated that the illicit income earned by Colombians from all drug sales:

1.   contributes approximately 6 percent to the nation's 30 percent annual inflation rate and 15–18 percent to the growth of its money supply

2. jeopardizes Colombia's financial institutions and renders precarious all forms of governmental economic planning
3. diverts large sums of governmental funds, which are needed elsewhere, to suppress growing and trafficking
4. contributes substantially to Colombia's becoming a food-importing country through the conversion of crop lands and rural laborers to drug production rather than that of staples
5. shrinks the pool of money available for legitimate lending and raises credit rates to the point that borrowers turn to extralegal sources (often traffickers or their colleagues) to secure financing
6. contributes to increased tax evasion among a populace noted for not paying taxes
7. penetrates and/or gains control of legitimate private corporations
8. becomes the largest source of dollars in the underground economy and adds millions to the nation's foreign exchange surplus
9. grossly inflates the value of farm land, property, goods, services, and even art works in trafficking areas.[27]

One response of the López administration to the drug trade was the opening of a *ventanilla siniestra* ("left-handed" or "sinister" window) in the Banco de la República. At that window, anyone could exchange dollars for pesos—with no questions asked. Other dollars entered the economy through the long-flourishing black market for dollars (but with an unusual twist: soon dollars were worth *less* in the black market than they were in official exchange). Many other dollars were simply not brought into the country, but placed in banks and investments in other countries. This new, large supply of dollars was soon augmented by the highest coffee prices in Colombian history.

The Coffee "Bonanza." Average coffee prices in 1974 were US$0.78 a pound. This changed dramatically after a July frost in Brazil. Colombian coffee was sold for US$0.81 on an average in 1975, US$1.58 in 1976, and US$2.40 in 1977. While this increased foreign income normally would have been welcomed and did increase Colombia's foreign reserves quickly, it—together with the "other economy" dollars—increased the money supply too rapidly. Because the productive capacity of the economy was not similarly raised, inflation threatened to increase more than the 20–30 percent a year that had been common since the Pastrana presidency.

The López government's response was to withdraw some of the dollars from the economy. Import restrictions were loosened (thereby prejudicing Colombian manufactures to a degree); coffee taxes were increased; a waiting period for changing dollars at the full official rate was instituted; and governmental expenditures—to close the gaps that López had talked about, to develop hydroelectric power, and many other things—were either delayed or cancelled completely. In an irony of a dependent economy, Alfonso López Michelsen found that he could not close the gaps, not because of the lack of foreign exchange that had so characterized governments in the 1960s, but because there was too much foreign exchange.

The Turbay Government

In August 1978 Julio César Turbay Ayala inherited the problems faced by López, although by the end of Turbay's government both the coffee and drug bonanzas had ended. Like every recent president, he came up with a four-year plan, in his case called the "Plan of National Integration." The four specific goals of the plan were economic decentralization and regional autonomy, development of transportation and means of communication, development of the energy and mining sectors, and development of a new social strategy. An unstated goal of the Turbay government was the control of inflation. In this he notably failed, as inflation was 25–30 percent for each of the four years.

It is perhaps too early to fully evaluate the Turbay government, but some tentative conclusions can be given. Economic decentralization and regional autonomy were elusive. While the National Planning Department was supposed to give priority to investments outside of the four major cities, the change was not impressive. Most major decisions were still made in Bogotá. Investments in transportation and communication—as well as other projects—were carried out, but some were delayed because of the fear of fueling more inflation.

In the energy sector, the López programs were continued. All new petroleum agreements were in association contracts; by 1978 this had become almost one-quarter of the petroleum. In 1980 petroleum production went up dramatically for the first time in more than a decade; US$471 million were needed for petroleum imports in the same year, making Colombia a minor importer as compared to other Third World countries.

In September 1980 Turbay and the CONPES accepted INTERCOR's "commercial declaration" for the North Cerrejón region. This declaration, made after explorations proved that there was an economically feasible amount of coal, called for up-front investments of nearly US$3 billion in order to construct a strip mine, facilities, railroad, and port that would export a minimum of 15 million metric tonnes (16.5 million short tons) of coal a year beginning in 1986. There was almost immediately a national debate about the Cerrejón-North contract and the commercial declaration, a debate that was somewhat theoretical since the decision had already been made.[28] A key goal of both the López and Turbay governments was to develop another source of foreign exchange. During the López years this hardly seemed necessary (although one of his ministers told me that this goal was important, so as to avoid the "populism" of the late 1960s—the Rojas Pinilla popularity no doubt—and concurrent balance-of-payment difficulties and unemployment).[29] By 1980, however, people in Bogotá and Washington were talking about the "difficult times" for the Colombian economy until the coal would go on line in 1986. If one accepts Exxon's own figures, the Colombian government will earn, in taxes and royalties and on its own half of the coal, between US$48.852 billion (in current dollars, assuming production of 15 million metric tonnes [16.5 million short tons] a year and low prices for coal) and US$100.7 billion (in current dollars, assuming production of 25 million metric tonnes [27.6 million short tons] a year and high prices).[30]

In October 1979 a bidding was opened for the Central Cerrejón area. In May 1981 the award was given to a Spanish-Colombian consortium (Domi-Prodeco-Auxini). Under the terms of this "service" contract, production was to begin with 300,000 tonnes (330,800 short tons) in 1982, 700,000 tonnes (771,800 short tons) in 1983, and 1.5 million tonnes (1.65 million short tons) per year between 1984 and 1989. The consortium does all the investment, and CARBOCOL buys all the coal at the mine mouth. At this point, it apparently plans to use all or most of the Central Cerrejón coal in electricity plants on the Caribbean coast.[31]

By June 1981 the international coffee price was down to US$1.27 a pound; by a year later it had recovered to about US$1.40. In the same time period, earnings from the drug trade were also down, because of a coordinated program between the U.S. and Colombian governments, because other South American countries were producing cocaine from coca leaves, and because more marijuana was being grown in the United States.[32] So the last Turbay year and a half was characterized by declining balances of trade. Colombian international reserves increased slightly, reaching a point of US$5.633 billion at the end of 1981.

CONCLUSION

In 1980–1981 there was a general recession in the Colombian economy. Reasons for this downturn, in addition to low earnings from coffee and drugs, are no doubt multiple. Among the reasons are the following: First, wages for the majority of the people (especially those in the poor and middle sectors) had not kept up with inflation. In that circumstance, consumption declined. While average wages are still much lower in Colombia than in the United States (the minimum wage in 1982 was about US$100 a month), many prices in Bogotá were as high as or even higher than those in southern New England. This was particularly the case for clothing and some, but far from all, foodstuffs.

Second, often the legally imported foreign goods and illegal contraband were no more expensive than comparable Colombian goods. In that circumstance, many Colombians would buy the foreign goods on the assumption that they were better made. Third, because of the foreign exchange entering the country, the peso had been artificially high in value (that is to say, with a low exchange rate). Such a condition, while encouraging imports needed to cool off the inflation, also discouraged exports. Colombian textiles, formerly competitive in the world market, were no longer so.

Fourth, investments increasingly were going into those areas with good guarantees against inflation—real estate, construction, and financial speculation—rather than productive industry. Capital goods were becoming obsolete and hence not competitive in the world market (although it should be pointed out that "nonobsolete" capital goods would have been more capital intensive, which would have led to more unemployment). Finally, increasing protectionism in the industrial world made it more difficult to sell goods, especially industrial ones. At the same time, capital goods needed from the inflation-ridden developed world cost more each year.

At a more basic level, the 1980–1981 recession can be explained as a manifestation of economic dependency. The industrial world was in recession, so dependent Colombia would have to be also (unless it had something that the industrial world wanted terribly). The fragile Colombian economy does well when there is good, steady, moderate demand for its primary products (whether coffee or marijuana), but not so well when there is declining demand or even excessive demand. The economy never has been entirely outwardly oriented: A prosperous textile industry (for example) existed until badly harmed by exogenous factors—the need to import more to avoid inflation, higher salaries coming with inflation, an overvalued peso. But, as so often is the case in dependent Colombia, short-term considerations (controlling inflation) received priority over long-term development goals (such as protecting national industry).

NOTES

1. Carlos F. Diaz-Alejandro, *Foreign Trade Regimes and Economic Development: Colombia* (New York: National Bureau of Economic Research, 1976), pp. 5, 10.

2. Ibid., p. 5; *Atlas Básico de Colombia* (Bogotá: Instituto Geográfico "Augustín Codazzi," 1980), p. 6.

3. R. Albert Berry, "Colombia's Economic Situation and Prospects," Paper given at the U.S. State Department Conference on Colombia, November 9, 1981, p. 1.

4. Diaz-Alejandro, p. 92; División de Estudios Económicos, DANE, "El comercio exterior Colombiano en 1979," *Revista Mensual de Estadística*, 348 (Julio, 1980): 36; Daniel L. Premo, "U.S.-Colombian Relations: A Contemporary Perspective," mimeographed (Chestertown, Md.: Washington College, 1981), p. 18.

5. Quoted in Miguel Urrutia, *The Development of the Colombian Labor Movement* (New Haven: Yale University Press, 1969), pp. 6–7.

6. Francisco Leal Buitrago, "Social Classes, International Trade and Foreign Capital in Colombia: An Attempt at Historical Interpretation of the Formation of the State, 1819–1935," Ph.D. dissertation, University of Wisconsin, 1974, p. 196.

7. Confidential interview, *Estrategia* journalist, April 20, 1981.

8. A. Eugene Havens, William L. Flinn, and Susana Lastarria-Cornhill, "Agrarian Reform and the National Front: A Class Analysis," in R. Albert Berry, Ronald G. Hellman, and Mauricio Solaún, eds., *Politics of Compromise: Coalition Government in Colombia* (New Brunswick, N.J.: Transaction Books, 1980), p. 355.

9. Subcommittee on American Republics Affairs, Committee on Foreign Relations, U.S. Senate, *Survey of the Alliance for Progress, Colombia—A Case History of U.S. Aid* (Washington, D.C.: Government Printing Office, 1969), p. 121.

10. Diaz-Alejandro, pp. 29, 61–62.

11. Ibid., p. 37.

12. Francois J. Lombard, *The Foreign Investment Screening Process in LDCs: The Case of Colombia, 1967–1975* (Boulder, Colo.: Westview Press, 1979), p. 41.

13. Ibid., pp. 28–29.

14. Bruce Michael Bagley, "Political Power, Public Policy and the State in Colombia: Case Studies of the Urban and Agrarian Reforms during the National Front, 1958–1974," Ph.D. dissertation, University of California, Los Angeles, 1979, Chapter 3.

15. William Paul McGreevey, "Population Policy under the National Front," in Berry, Hellman, and Solaún, p. 418.

16. Ibid., pp. 418–410. McGreevey argues that the National Front, which brought the church behind both parties, made this policy possible.

17. Bagley, Chapter 5.

18. Ibid.

19. Quoted in John Sheahan, *Aspects of Planning and Development in Colombia*, Technical Papers Series no. 10 (Austin, Tex.: The Institute of Latin American Studies, 1977), pp. 23–24.

20. Malcolm Gillis and Charles E. McLure, Jr., "The 1974 Colombian Tax Reform and Income Distribution," in R. Albert Berry and Ronald Soligo, eds., *Economic Policy and Income Distribution in Colombia* (Boulder, Colo.: Westview Press, 1980), pp. 47–48.

21. Ministerio de Minas y Energía, *Bases para un plan energético nacional* (Bogotá: n.p., 1977), Table 16.

22. Confidential interview, former ECOPETROL official, April 24, 1981.

23. Ministerio de Minas y Energía, Table 16.

24. Jorge Villegas, *Petróleo, Oligarquía e Imperio* (Bogotá: Ediciones E.S.E., 1969), *passim*.

25. A more complete account is Harvey F. Kline, "The Coal of 'El Cerrejón': An Historical Analysis of Major Colombian Policy Decisions and MNC Activities," *Inter-American Economic Affairs* 35 (Winter 1981): 69–90.

26. Richard B. Craig, "Domestic Implications of Illicit Drug Cultivation, Processing, and Trafficking in Colombia," Paper given at the U.S. State Department Conference on Colombia, November 9, 1981, pp. 4–5.

27. Ibid.

28. Harvey F. Kline, *Energy Policy and the Colombian Elite: A Synthesis and Interpretation*, Occasional Paper no. 4, The Center for Hemisphere Studies (Washington, D.C.: American Enterprise Institute, 1982). Also *Exxon and Colombian Coal: An Analysis of the North Cerrejón Debates*, Occasional Papers Series no. 14 (Amherst: Program in Latin American Studies, University of Massachusetts at Amherst, 1982).

29. Confidential interview, former minister of *hacienda*, April 20, 1981.

30. Calculated from INTERCOR, "Commercial Declaration" (July 1, 1980), Appendix V, Table 1.

31. Confidential interview, CARBOCOL official, June 4, 1981.

32. Craig, p. 6.

6

The International Dimension

Rarely do international issues play an important part in Colombian domestic politics. In part this is because of the relative weakness of foreign multinational corporations. Although there are MNCs in the country, the economy is not so dominated by them as other Latin American countries have been (Cuba before the Castro revolution, for example); neither is the major export product controlled by a few foreign businesses (as Chilean copper was dominated by Kennecott and Anaconda before 1970). In part the unimportance of foreign issues is because, since the early years of this century, relations between the Colombian government and the U.S. government have been at least cordial, if not friendly.

Yet there is no reason to deny that Colombia is a relatively small and poor country in a hemisphere dominated by the United States, in both governmental and economic terms. This unequal power relationship can be shown through briefly contrasting the Colombian "foreign-policy" establishment with the U.S. governmental presence in the South American country.

The best, and simplest, description of the Colombian foreign-policy establishment is that it is weak and diffuse. "Foreign" policy is made not only in the foreign-affairs ministry, but also in PROEXPO (if the issue is exports), INCOMEX (imports), or the ministry of the treasury (foreign loans and finance). The negotiation of foreign treaties dealing with the most important Colombian export, coffee, is handled by FEDECAFE—an amazing indication of the extent of "privatization" of Colombian politics. The Colombian military has a separate network of information and communications. The official assigned to be liaison with the U.S. Drug Enforcement Agency does *not* work out of the Colombian embassy in Washington (which has only about five officials other than clerical and maintenance staff).[1]

In contrast, the predominant power of the hemisphere—the United States—has a large, centralized foreign-affairs establishment in Colombia. There are approximately 200 officials in the block-square embassy in Bogotá (which Colombian "myth" has it was constructed completely with materials imported from the United States and includes secret escape tunnels). These officials include foreign-service officers, Drug Enforcement Agency people, military attaches, and even officials of the Agency for International Development (at least still in 1981, although AID programs had been ended, at Colombian request, in 1975). In addition there are consulates in Medellín, Cali, and Barranquilla.

Despite the size of this staff—plus the number of Colombia experts in government agencies in Washington, D.C.—there appears (at least to me) to be no clear-cut policy regarding Colombia on the part of the U.S. government. Rather, U.S. policy seems to be reactive to events within Colombia that affect the United States directly (drugs, for example) and to outside events that impinge on the Andean country. For example, subversion within Colombia (which has been fought, at least since the early 1960s, with U.S. counterinsurgency assistance) is seen as important because it is part of a Cuban plan to destabilize the area.

This chapter describes the history of Colombian political relations with the outside world and discusses current foreign relations of the country, both political and economic. In the conclusion I will put forward an explanation of why foreign affairs seem to be so unimportant to Colombian domestic politics.

HISTORICAL BACKGROUND

In general the history of Colombian foreign policy is an uneventful one, despite certain notable exceptions. This was particularly the case in the nineteenth century. The only notable occurrence was the 1826 ill-fated Congress of Panamá, but it should be remembered that the "Colombia" that called for this congress was Gran Colombia and that the "Colombian" leader instrumental in calling the conference was the Venezuelan Simón Bolívar. Foreign economic policy was explicitly designed to exchange Colombian primary products for European (and later U.S.) manufactured goods.

From the Loss of Panamá to the Alliance for Progress

Probably the most important events of Colombian foreign policy came in 1903 when the U.S. government aided and abetted a rebellion in the *departamento* of Panamá (which no doubt never had been effectively integrated into the economic and political life of the nation). The isthmus had been used for transit for a number of years, and in 1846 the United

States and Colombia had signed a treaty for such transit. A railroad had been built.

It was only after the Spanish-American War that the United States government turned seriously to the question of a canal. For a while there was a debate over whether Mexico, Nicaragua, or Panamá would be the location, the choice being made for the last. A treaty was then negotiated between the United States and Colombia. This Hay-Herrán Treaty stipulated that Colombia would receive a payment of US$10 million for the rights to build the canal, plus (after 10 years) an annual payment of US$250,000. The canal would be built on a strip of land 10 kilometers (6.2 miles) in width, and there was a positive guarantee of Colombian sovereignty over the zone thus created. The treaty was for 100 years.

Troubles between the two countries began when the Colombian senate (meeting after the War of the Thousand Days) failed to ratify the treaty. Some of the Colombian senators feared a loss of sovereignty; others argued that the payments were not large enough. The U.S. government's reaction was clear. The secretary of state sent a message to the U.S. ambassador, who faithfully passed it on: the Colombians should pass the treaty without delay, exactly as it was negotiated. This was the coup de grâce for the treaty, as the U.S. message said, in effect, that the Colombian senate, one of the Latin American legislative branches with the most tradition of debate, should not debate. The treaty was not ratified.

Theodore Roosevelt, speaking not so softly, responded with two alternatives. One was the possibility of choosing Nicaragua for the canal. The other was "In some way or shape to interfere when it becomes necessary to secure the Panama route without further dealings with the foolish and homicidal corruptionists in Bogotá."[2] The opportunity came soon, and the "big stick" was brought out. On November 2, 1903, there was a revolt in Panamá, apparently instigated by the Frenchman Philippe Bunau-Varilla, who had a large investment in the company with the concession to build the canal (although Colombian historian Germán Arciniegas suggests that the U.S. government had prior knowledge).[3] U.S. war ships prevented the transit of Colombian troops who were sent to put down the revolt. Events then went with lightning speed for the early twentieth century:

- November 4: Panama declared its independence.
- November 6: The U.S. government recognized Panama.
- November 13: Bunau-Varilla arrived in Washington to negotiate.

- November 15: Secretary of State John Hay gave Bunau-Varilla a draft treaty.
- November 17: Bunau-Varilla returned a final draft to Hay.
- November 18: the treaty was signed.

So in a period of seventeen days, the Panama incident was over. Both Bunau-Varilla and Roosevelt later received international awards (TR the Nobel Prize in 1906), and the U.S. president later said, "I took the Canal Zone, started the Canal, and then left the [U.S.] Congress not to debate the Canal, but to debate me."[4] It is little wonder that many Colombians are still sensitive about the incident, as shown in 1964 when the U.S. government proposed, among other alternatives, another canal in the Atrato River area of Colombia. An entire generation of Colombians in high school learned their history from a text that concluded its section on the topic with the charge that they, the youth, must rectify their history and used the stirring phrase, "At that time, the cry that Bolívar made, inspired by his genius, 'Long Live the God of Colombia!' will be mixed with another, more sonorous and extensive, that will make the ashes of Montezuma boil again and will give heat and life to the steppes of Patagonia—'Long live the God of Latin America!' "[5]

Yet no nationalist movement (such as those later to be very important in Panama itself) was organized in Colombia. One explanation is simply that the opposition party (the Liberals), which might have led this nationalism, was not able to because of the decimation of the War of the Thousand Days. This general theme—nationalism at the personal level but lack of organized nationalist movements—has continued until today.

While there might have been a "chill" in Colombian-U.S. relations in the following years, the Conservative presidents of the period faced a clear economic fact: the Colombian economy increasingly depended on export earnings from coffee, and the principal customer for that period was the United States. Conservative President Marco Fidel Suárez (1918–1921) dignified this relationship when he proclaimed the "doctrine of the Polar Star," by which he meant that his country should look northward, to the powerful United States, both as an example of social and political democracy and as a partner, with whom Colombia's destinies were inextricably linked for reasons of geographic proximity and complementary economies.[6] Despite some of the contretemps mentioned below, this doctrine (although not in the same rhetorical terms) has guided Colombian foreign policy ever since.

In 1922 the U.S. Senate ratified the Thompson-Urrutia Treaty. Colombia had accepted it soon after its negotiation in 1914. Under this treaty, Colombia was awarded an indemnity of US$25 million for the loss of Panama. Why the U.S. Senate waited so long to ratify seems to be explained by two factors. One, the continuing presence of Theodore Roosevelt, who called the treaty a crime against the United States, ended with his death in 1919. The other prerequisite for approval seems to have been favorable petroleum contracts for Standard Oil of New Jersey, which had entered the country in 1920.

Foreign policy events since Panama have been few. They include the following incidents. In 1924 Colombia won a diplomatic triumph in securing from Peru a boundary settlement that gave her Leticia (see Figure 1.1), in the extreme southeast part of the country. This gave Colombia a port on the Amazon River and hence an outlet to the Atlantic. In 1932, a group of Peruvian irregulars from Iquitos seized the small town, thus threatening war between the two countries. Colombia took the matter to the League of Nations, which scolded Peru. No war eventuated.

During World War II Colombia's policies were unabashedly pro–United States. It was during the immediate prewar and early wartime years that institutionalized military, financial, and technical cooperation arrangements between the United States and Colombia began. Colombia has continued to be a faithful member of inter-American organizations. It is perhaps appropriate that the Organization of American States (OAS) was set up at the 1948 Bogotá Conference (during the *Bogotazo*) and that the first secretary general of the OAS was Alberto Lleras Camargo. Further, in the San Francisco Conference of 1945, Colombia was one of the more prominent Latin American participants. The country's representatives fought against the big power veto in the Security Council and for a recognized role for regional organizations in the UN Charter.[7]

Colombia was the only Latin American nation to contribute troops to the UN action in Korea. While the Laureano Gómez government might have been motivated by support of the international organization, the sending of troops also reflected the very close relationship that Colombia had developed with the United States. Further, since this action occurred during *La Violencia*, there are even rumors that the first Colombian battalion sent to Korea largely consisted of Liberal troops whom the Conservative administration wanted to keep at a safe distance.[8]

The Alliance for Progress in Colombia

By the time that John F. Kennedy announced the Alliance for Progress on March 13, 1961, Colombian political leaders already for a decade had been calling for a massive assistance program. Carlos Lleras Restrepo, for example, was one of three experts (along with Eduardo Frei and Raúl Prebisch) who were charged with the preparation of the

1954 inter-American economic conference; proposals of that conference were strikingly similar to the Alliance for Progress of seven years later. Further, Colombia already had adopted a land-reform program (at least on paper), one of the explicit goals of the Alliance for Progress.

Colombia was soon chosen as one of the "showcases" of the alliance, not only because it had land reform in place but also because it had a vigorous private sector, a relatively enlightened political elite, a large industrial base, and many of the typical social and economic problems of Latin America—rapid population growth, a primitive school system, overreliance on one commodity for foreign exchange, and a maldistribution of land and income. The Colombian elite responded, and the country was the first in the Americas to produce a comprehensive plan, a prerequisite for Alliance for Progress assistance.

During the Alliance for Progress years, the U.S. government probably had more influence in Colombian domestic politics than ever before—or since. In 1961–1967 U.S. aid was US$732 million (US$491 million of which was alliance aid administered through AID), and by 1974 the total had reached US$1.4 billion. These monies, closely supervised by AID officials in Bogotá, went into land reform, education, health, housing, transportation, and electricity.

There is little doubt that many Colombians benefited from the projects funded by the Alliance for Progress. A report of the Subcommittee on American Republics Affairs of the Committee on Foreign Relations of the U.S. Senate saw benefits as summarized in Table 6.1. But there were "negative externalities" also: capital-intensive machinery was imported, the tied loans of the alliance encouraged more trade with the United States, and the country's debt burden increased. Indeed the same U.S. Senate report concluded that U.S. aid to Colombia made it possible for the Colombian government to postpone making more basic reforms in such fields as public administration, taxation, local government, education, and agriculture. The report concluded that, without alliance aid, the Colombian government either would have moved more rapidly than it did or would have faced a revolution. The first of the two alternatives was seen as more likely.[9] While short- and medium-term perception might be that the Alliance for Progress was a success, one might ask if the Colombian poor would agree.

In 1975 President Alfonso López M. announced that Colombia would relinquish U.S. economic assistance; thus ended the role that the Agency for International Development had enjoyed since the Alliance. López went out of his way to emphasize that cordial economic relations with the United States existed, but also stated that "foreign aid breeds an unhealthy economic dependency and delays or undermines measures that should be taken for development."[10] A U.S. diplomat in Colombia

Table 6.1
Quantitative Indicators Change in Colombia During Alliance For Progress

Indicator	Pre-Alliance	Alliance
Per capita Gross National Product[a]	US$276	US$295
Land Reform[b]		
Farms over 100 hectares (latifundios)		
% of farms	3.5%	2.7%
% of total land	66.0%	58.9%
Farms under 5 hectares (minifundios)		
% of farms	62.5%	71.4%
% of total land	4.5%	6.3%
Education, percentage of age group in school[c]		
primary	59.9%	69.6%
secondary	10.8%	16.4%
post-secondary	1.7%	2.7%
	RATE OF	CHANGE[d]
Number of physicians/10,000 people	11.4%	10.3%
Nurses trained annually	38.6%	35.4%
Life expectancy at birth	8.5%	16.3%
Death rate	-11.3%	-14.6%
Infant mortality	-10.4%	-11.8%
Increase in paved roads	21.2%	4.9%
Increase in gravel roads	28.6%	11.0%
Increase in installed KWH	10.8%	32.8%

Source: Subcommittee on American Republics Affairs, Committee on Foreign Relations, U.S. Senate, Survey of the Alliance for Progress: Colombia--a Case History of U.S. Aid (Washington: Government Printing Office, 1969), passim.

[a] Pre-Alliance: 1961; Alliance: 1967
[b] Pre-Alliance: 1960; Alliance: 1967
[c] Pre-Alliance: 1961; Alliance: 1966
[d] Pre-Alliance: average annual increase, 1958-1961; Alliance: average annual increase, 1962-66

later complained to me that the embassy had lost all "leverage" with
the end of AID monies. Perhaps influence did indeed decrease for him
and his colleagues, but surely it did not completely disappear.

The Andean Pact

Perhaps the boldest Colombian initiative in foreign matters came
in the 1960s when the government, along with that of Chile, was
instrumental in the instigation of the Andean Common Market (commonly called the Andean Pact). In part the idea resulted from impatience
with the slow development of a larger common market through the
Latin American Free Trade Association (LAFTA), but rather than replacing
LAFTA, the Andean Pact was to be a subregional group within it. The
concept was first expressed in the "Declaration of Bogotá" in August
1966 and was formalized in the "Agreement of Cartagena" in May
1969.

The original members of the Andean Pact were Bolivia, Chile,
Colombia, Ecuador, and Peru. Venezuela joined in 1973; Chile withdrew
in 1975. The pact had (and to a degree still has) seven major goals.

The first was trade liberalization: all trade barriers between the
pact countries would be eliminated by the end of 1980, with Bolivia
and Ecuador having an additional five years. A Common External Tariff,
applicable to imports from outside the subregion, was a second goal.
These common import duties were to apply by 1980. A third goal was
a sectoral program of industrial development. Long lists of which country
would produce which goods were drawn up. (Once, during a short visit
in Colombia, I stayed with some friends. During a Sunday afternoon
social gathering with relatives and friends, they decided that they should
leave their bureaucratic and teaching jobs for more lucrative careers in
industry. One fetched the list of manufactured goods that Colombia
had under the Andean Pact, and it was quickly decided that their talents
fitted with the country's designation as the only one of the pact that
could manufacture crutches and wheel chairs.) A fourth goal was
economic policy harmonization, so that there would be common laws
on such things as unfair trade practices, industrial promotion, tourist
transit by automobile, and others. A fifth goal was the creation of a
development finance institution (the Andean Development Corporation),
which would have capital from all member countries and from international loans.

No doubt the best known and most controversial goal of the
Andean Pact was to have a common policy (an Andean Foreign
Investment Code) on all investors who were not nations or residents
of the member states. This "Decision 24," adopted in 1971, defined as
"foreign firms" those that had less than 51 percent of the capital in

the hands of nationals; "mixed companies" were those having between 51 and 80 percent local capital; "national," those having 81 percent or more local capital. Foreign companies that existed prior to December 31, 1971, and that intended to take advantage of tariff reductions had to declare their intention of becoming mixed enterprises. For new foreign enterprises, gradual conversion to "mixed" status was mandatory, whether they intended to sell in the subregional market or not. Firms intending to export 80 percent or more of their production out of the subregion were exempt from the rule. The reduction of foreign ownership had to be effected within fifteen years in Chile, Colombia, Peru, and Venezuela and within twenty-two in Bolivia and Ecuador. Direct foreign investment would not be authorized in areas already adequately covered by local investors, and the purchase of local companies would not be allowed. Foreign investors would remit no more than 14 percent of their investments. No direct foreign investment in insurance companies or banks would be authorized, and foreign banks would have to offer at least 80 percent of their capital to local investors within a three-year period if they wanted to receive local deposits. Decision 24, however, did not apply to petroleum or mining. It was suggested in those areas that the form of contract be "joint venture," and that any concessions be short-term ones.

The seventh goal of the Andean Pact concerned the possibility of creating "Andean Multinational Enterprises." The pact decreed that national investors from the Andean countries would be subject to the provisions of Decision 24 *unless* they formed such an enterprise, defined as one in which a minimum block of 15 percent of the share capital came from at least two member countries.

The results of the Andean Pact have been mixed. The trade between the individual nations has increased, and there has been some specialization of manufacturing industry. Notable successes in Andean Multinational Enterprises include Monómeros Colombo-Venezolanos, a Colombian and Venezuelan petrochemical joint venture (which was founded even before Venezuela joined the pact). One reform in Colombia, which followed the spirit if not the letter of the pact, was the "Colombianization" of the foreign banks. By decree in early 1975 the López government set up a commission to study the question; opposition from the foreign banks, but support from Colombian banks, was soon found. Although the Andean Pact stated that foreign banks would have to offer at least 80 percent of the stock to residents of the country, the final law, as approved by the congress in December 1975, stated that Colombians would have to be offered 51 percent of the capital. In effect, they were to become "mixed" enterprises rather than "national" ones.

Figure 6.1 An Andean MNC: Monómeros Colombo-Venezolanos

During the three years that the law allowed, the foreign banks sold 51 percent of their capital (First National City Bank became the Banco Internacional de Colombia, for example, as all changed their names in so doing). Critics from the Left, however, argue that the total capital was also doubled, or more, in the process: for example, the First National City Bank had, before the law became effective, paid capital of US$200 million. The Banco Internacional de Colombia had total paid capital of US$448 million. As 49 percent of this latter figure (US$219.5 million) is greater than the "un-Colombianized" bank's paid capital, the critics argue that the López "Colombianization" did not make the country less dependent on foreign banks.[11]

There also have been notable problems with the Andean Pact. For one thing, several nations (Colombia included) adopted laws instituting the pact that made exceptions to the rules originally agreed upon. For another, transportation difficulties in the Andean region remained an impediment.

Perhaps the most notable difficulty came from the change of governments in the region and their different views, especially about Decision 24. In 1973 the Pinochet military dictatorship replaced the socialist Allende in Chile; in 1980, the democratically elected Belaúnde in Peru called for changes in the pact agreed upon by more progressive military governments in his country.

In Colombia, even in the absence of such dramatic changes of government, there have been some second thoughts about the stipulations of the Andean Pact. The government of Carlos Lleras Restrepo was, no doubt, the most reformist of recent years. Although the Foreign Investment Code did not go that far beyond Decree-Law 444, it was opposed by private groups in Colombia, especially ANDI and other business groups, since the Code gave "first refusal" to the respective governments in purchasing the stock to be divested by foreign MNCs. The opposition remains: in November 1981 an *antioqueño* industrialist argued that Decision 24 prevented more foreign capital from coming in, capital that he thought would help the country.[12] In the same week, I heard a U.S. businessman argue that there were two negative factors, along with many positive ones, in Colombia—the crime problem in major Colombian cities and the bureaucratic hassle of complying with Decision 24.

CURRENT COLOMBIAN FOREIGN RELATIONS

There are today, as in the past, three separate dimensions of Colombian relations with foreign "actors": intergovernmental relations, economic relations with foreign private "actors" (MNCs, primarily), and relations with international lending agencies. In this section I will discuss all of these, as of mid-1982.

Intergovernmental Relations

It appears that Colombian ties with the U.S. government have become closer in the past two years than before. This has been in part because of the drug trade; in part because of problems that Colombia has, or might in the future have, with Cuba, Nicaragua, and Venezuela. In the latter case, the Colombian government looked to the United States as a close ally.

During the Alfonso López administration, the U.S. government seemed much more concerned with the drug activities than the Colombian government was. López saw the problem as one caused by the consumption of marijuana and cocaine in the United States, rather than by its production in Colombia. As he stated in 1975, "These are North American citizens, with North American capital, with North American registered airplanes, that take off from North American airports to convert us into a drug trafficking platform."[13] This attitude (along with certain other circumstantial evidence) led some people to conclude that López himself had some connections with the drug *mafioso*.

The Turbay administration played a more active (and cooperative) role in the control of drug production than the López government had, despite rumors that some of Turbay's relatives were involved. This change of direction might have been because of the growing realization of the distortions that the illicit trade was bringing to the economy, as well as increasing drug problems among Colombians. For whatever reason, the Turbay government signed a drug-control agreement with the United States, involving additional security measures in the Guajira area. For the first time the Colombian military took over responsibility for drug interdiction (the National Police had this duty earlier) and soon placed the Guajira region under military jurisdiction. The U.S. government provided Colombia with US$3.8 million under the international narcotics program; the National Police, who had resumed primary responsibility in 1980, soon were seizing three times more marijuana and six times more cocaine than that seized in the United States.[14] In February 1982 U.S. Attorney General William French claimed that, in fourteen months of the joint U.S.-Colombian operation (code named "Tiburón" or "Shark"), 2,594 tonnes (2,860 tons) of marijuana had been seized and more than 500 people arrested. It is of note that most of the marijuana was seized in Colombia, while most of the arrests were made in the U.S.[15]

Colombian bilateral relations with three Latin American countries—Nicaragua, Cuba, and Venezuela—also led to closer relations with the United States. This was especially true in the first two cases, in which Colombia and the United States shared apparent common "enemies."

Disputes with Nicaragua. In the case of Nicaragua the point of contention has been the status of the islands of San Andrés and Providencia and the uninhabited keys of Quita Sueño, Roncador, and Serrana. This dispute dates back to 1803, when the reefs and islands were taken away from the capitancy general of Guatemala and placed under the viceroyalty of Nueva Granada. In 1828 Colombia and Nicaragua signed a treaty in which Colombia recognized Nicaragua's claims to its eastern seaboard (which had also been placed under Nueva Granada's jurisdiction in 1803) in return for Colombian sovereignty over the keys under dispute. Colombia's claims to San Andrés and Providencia are based on a treaty between the two nations in 1928, not ratified by Nicaragua until 1950. The 1928 treaty did not mention the three keys because they were the subject of litigation between the United States and Colombia. The United States renounced all claims to the reefs in a 1972 treaty, at which point the Somoza dynasty government of Nicaragua issued a formal statement reiterating its claims to Quita Sueño, Roncador, and Serrana.[16] Colombia ratified the 1972 treaty in 1973, but it was not until late 1981 that the U.S. Senate did so.

In late 1979 the new Sandinista government in Nicaragua reasserted its claim to the keys and the two islands, claiming that Nicaragua's 1928 treaty with Colombia was invalid because it was signed under duress during the U.S. military occupation of Nicaragua. Colombia's response was to increase its naval and air patrols of the reefs and to construct a new military base on San Andrés.[17] The plot thickened when, in March 1982, the governments of the United States and Colombia "discussed" (but did not "negotiate") the possibility of a U.S. base on San Andrés. Given the proximity to Nicaragua, these discussions did nothing to reduce the tension between the two Latin American countries.

Relations with Cuba. Relations with Cuba have been soured by alleged training of Colombian guerrillas on that island. In 1962 the Colombian government went along with the Rio Treaty nations' vote to end diplomatic relations with Cuba and did not reestablish diplomatic ties until 1975. In March 1981, following an M-19 invasion of southern Nariño, the Turbay government broke those ties because some of the guerrillas stated that they had been trained in Cuba. This accusation was not denied by the Cuban ambassador before his departure. Tensions have persisted since that date. In October 1981 President Turbay stated that there was an "international plot against the democratic regimes of the continent, coordinated by Cuba but inspired by other powers."[18] In January 1982 Foreign Minister Carlos Lemos Simmonds added that "Cuba has connections with the drug traffickers and through them sends arms to the armed groups."[19] The U.S. government, likewise, stated at various times in 1981 and 1982 that Colombia was one of the victims of Cuban aggression.

Venezuelan Issues. Bilateral relations with Venezuela are different in at least three important ways: both nations are allies of the United States, Colombian-Venezuelan hostilities are deep-seated (Venezuelans consider all *colombianos* to be thieves and/or prostitutes; Colombians consider all *venezolanos* to be gauche nouveaux riches who speak bad Spanish), and the questions in contention are potentially more important than those disputed with Nicaragua and Cuba. In essence, there are two issues separating the two Andean nations. The first has to do with the thousands (some estimates are as high as 1 million) of Colombians who are illegally living in Venezuela. The situation is not unlike that between Mexico and the United States: The Colombians do menial jobs that others might not; Venezuela is a prosperous "safety valve" for Colombia. Given the long border that the two nations share, it is practically impossible to stop illegal Colombian migration to Venezuela.

The second issue has to do precisely with the border. Since 1970 there have been attempts to negotiate an off-shore boundary between the two countries, efforts that were suspended in 1980. The boundary in question is in the Gulf of Venezuela, thought to have petroleum.

Further, some Venezuelans have stated that the on-shore border between the Colombian Guajira *departamento* and the Venezuelan state of Zulia, a boundary that in part is an imaginary straight line, should be renegotiated. This issue has greater importance for Colombians than in the past because of the Cerrejón coal deposits.

In this context seemingly small incidents are blown out of proportion. During the 1981 Christmas festive season, for example, a Colombian band was jailed in Venezuela for playing a "pop" version of the Venezuelan national anthem. Later a group of Venezuelan musicians suffered a kind of revenge in Colombia. More seriously, Colombian leaders worry about the F-16 fighters that the United States sold to Venezuela, although then Secretary of State Alexander Haig assured them that the fighters would not be used against Colombia.

Given the concatenation of these three bilateral problems, it is not surprising that Colombia and the United States have, at this writing, a very close relationship. And, given the potential Colombian problems with the Caribbean keys, San Andrés, Providencia, the Guajira peninsula, and the Gulf of Venezuela off-shore boundary, it is little wonder that the foreign minister from Bogotá was one of the three Latin American supporters of the U.S. position during the Malvinas (Falklands) debates of May–June 1982.

The International Political Economy

As does every country, Colombia has a related set of international relations concerning its place in the international political economy. Foreign "actors" who play roles in this context include the multinational corporations, the multilateral lending agencies (especially the World Bank and the Inter-American Development Bank), the International Monetary Fund (IMF), and the United Nations.

Multinational corporations. The importance of MNCs in Colombia has never been so great as in some other Latin American countries. One study in the mid-1970s presented data that indicated that Colombia was seventh in MNC investment in the area (despite being, at the time, fourth in population), behind Brazil, Mexico, Venezuela, Panama, Peru, and Argentina. Only 3.9 percent of the MNC investment in Latin America in 1975 went to Colombia (and only 0.5 percent of MNC world investment).[20] The investment was US$648 million in 1975, while new investment approved was US$67 million in 1978, US$235 million in 1979, and US$1.396 billion in 1980. Most of the investment in this last year (US$1.249 billion) was Exxon's contribution to the North Cerrejón project. Foreign investment hence was 90 percent in mining, 8.5 percent in manufacturing, and 1.5 percent in financial institutions.[21]

Some additional detail should be presented along with these overall figures. First, foreign investment tends to be in certain sectors, and, some Colombian radicals would argue, it tends to be in the most profitable ones. Second, foreign trademarks are sold to Colombian firms—at a cost. Hence Colombians might purchase Levi's, Wrangler, Lee, Manhattan, Arrow, Van Heusen, Bobby Brooks, BVD, Jockey, Pierre Cardin, or Yves St. Laurent apparel (to mention some available in 1978) made by Colombian firms. But those firms charge more for such brands, pay a license fee to the foreign country, and, in some cases, might sell the same product without the foreign name for less.[22] This is a reflection of a common Colombian view that, if a product is foreign, even in name, it must be of better quality. (This is also a reason for the thriving contraband trade in the country.) Third, there is some evidence that several foreign firms, particularly in pharmaceuticals and rubber products, have participated in "transfer pricing." Through this juggling of accounts, which is at least possible for vertically integrated MNCs, stipulations such as profit-remittance limits can be ignored.

Finally, there is an active role that the U.S. Embassy plays in the increasing influence of MNCs. After a talk I had given, during which I criticized certain practices of MNCs, a U.S. diplomat told me that he disagreed with me: "What this country needs is more multinational corporations, not fewer. The Colombians are not capable of doing anything by themselves."[23] The same embassy serves as the location for U.S. businesses that come to Colombia to sell their wares. In late 1980, further, one representative of the U.S. Department of Energy spoke in Bogotá, sponsored by the embassy; when asked what the Colombians should do about the liquefaction and gasification of coal, he replied, "Watch what the U.S. companies are doing and choose the technology which suits your needs most."[24]

It is only among the Colombian "radicals" that such questions as appropriate technology (which for Colombia would be more labor intensive) are discussed. Among the leaders of the country, there are common assumptions that foreign MNCs are needed because of Colombia's lack of capital, technology, and know-how, which are gladly accepted from foreign MNCs. All of this contributes to a kind of national "inferiority complex" among the country's leaders, best summarized by the common expression *no somos capaces* ("We can't do it").

Multilateral Agencies. A final set of "actors" is the multilateral agencies—the IMF, World Bank, Inter-American Development Bank (IDB), and the United Nations. The first two are commonly perceived to be most important. In 1966, for example, there was a major confrontation between President Lleras Restrepo and the IMF over the latter's insistence that there be a major devaluation of the peso. The World Bank has had major funding programs for Colombia for the past twenty years, particularly in the hydroelectricity field. Critics of the bank insist that one reason for large increases in electricity rates has been the bank's insistence that they approximate international prices, despite "real" costs.

In early 1981 there was a debate over whether the country was becoming too much in debt, through new loans from the World Bank, the IDB, bilateral loans, and loans from private banks. One side stated that Colombia was the fifth largest debtor in the world, with the total foreign debt rising from US$2.350 billion in 1975 to US$3.9 billion in 1980. The government replied that the total foreign debt was less than the country's international reserves (which were about US$5.5 billion) and that the debt service for 1981 would be US$777.1 million, or only 13.2 percent of the country's exports. Further, the chief of the National Planning Department stated that the debt service for 1986 would be only 19 percent of the projected exports, still below the 20–25 percent that international lending agencies consider the maximum.[25]

What seems to be the case is that no single lending agency now has the "leverage" that the U.S. Agency for International Development had during the Alliance for Progress years. Colombia receives foreign loans from a multiplicity of sources, including multilateral banks, private banks in the United States and western Europe, and export promotion agencies of the governments of the United States, Germany, Canada, and the Soviet Union, among others.

These loans are possible simply because Colombia's credit rating is so good (some Colombians even argue that it is the best in the Third World). This was dramatically stated by the president of the Inter-American Development Bank in April 1981, "I always have said in every forum where the general situation in Latin America is analyzed, that there is a rare country among us, a country that in its monetary reserves has the equivalent of all of its public debt; I mean that it is a country that has completely open credit, that has not begun to use it, and that country is called Colombia."[26]

In the same time period, even Colombian critics of the World Bank and the IMF (not all of whom are radicals) had to change their opinions. This change came when it became public information that, at the initiative of the World Bank, the Colombian government asked for a loan from the United Nations in order to pay for international consultants to assist the National Coal Company (CARBOCOL). As it turned out, these consultants (supervised by the World Bank and paid by the United Nations) played a role in CARBOCOL's attempts to keep Exxon honest in the North Cerrejón project.

CONCLUSIONS:
COLOMBIA IN THE INTERNATIONAL ARENA

As this chapter has shown, Colombia has not been strongly anti–United States in its international policy—even after the loss of Panamá. In economic relations—although there are occasional conflicts, such as with the IMF in 1966—Colombian governments have gone along with the conditions placed by international lending agencies and have welcomed foreign businesses. Some leaders have even proudly declared that no foreign business interest has ever been nationalized, unless one counts the "Colombianization" of the banks. The final question of this chapter is why this is the case.

I believe the answer to be simple and to be part of the general "economic dependency" argument: Colombian political leaders are products of a class system. From economic dependency, it is possible that Colombia has lost as compared to a more nationalist policy (although such is the stuff for years of counterfactual conditional arguments that can never be proved empirically). But even if "Colombia" has lost, that does not mean that the upper class *colombianos* have. Quite well off, trained many times in U.S. universities (one Colombian friend once told me, "Just because Milton Friedman is a *gringo* don't be so naive to think that we don't have 'Chicago School boys' here also."), and the leaders of both political parties, these economic elites are doing very well, thank you, and have never had reasons to use nationalism as a tool for garnering votes.

So we are back to the multiclass political parties as an explanation, in this case of foreign policy. The fact is that recently only the Colombian Communist party (which at most gets about 1 percent of the vote) and the Rojas ANAPO (for a while) have used foreign-policy issues in electoral campaigns. The Liberals and Conservatives—with their popular bases made secure in other ways—have rarely tried to turn to new methods of winning votes—such as an anti-U.S. populist tactic.

NOTES

1. Daniel L. Premo, "U.S.-Colombian Relations: A Contemporary Perspective," mimeographed (Chestertown, Md.: Washington College, 1981), p. 2.

2. Federico Gil, *Latin American–United States Relations* (New York: Harcourt Brace Jovanovich, 1971), p. 126.

3. Germán Arciniegas, *Biografía del Caribe* (Buenos Aires: Editorial Sudamericana, 1963), p. 430.

4. Gil, p. 128.

5. Jesús María Henao and Gerardo Arrubla, *Historia de Colombia*, 8th ed. (Bogotá: Talleres Editoriales de la Librería Voluntad, 1967), p. 818.

6. David Bushnell, "Colombia" in Harold Eugene Davis, Larman C. Wilson, and others, *Latin American Foreign Policies: An Analysis* (Baltimore: The Johns Hopkins University Press, 1975), p. 407.

7. Ibid., p. 409.

8. Daniel L. Premo, "The Armed Forces and Colombian Politics: In Search of a Mission," mimeographed (Chestertown, Md.: Washington College, 1981), p. 9.

9. Subcommittee on American Republics Affairs, Committee on Foreign Relations, U.S. Senate, *Survey of the Alliance for Progress: Colombia—A Case History of U.S. Aid* (Washington, D.C.: Government Printing Office, 1969), p. 5.

10. Quote in Premo, "U.S.-Colombian Relations . . . ," p. 22.

11. Julio Silva Colmenares, *Los Verdaderos Dueños del País* (Bogotá: Fondo Editorial Suramérica, 1977), p. 152.

12. *El Espectador* (Bogotá), November 8, 1981.

13. Quoted in Richard B. Craig, "Domestic Implications of Illicit Drug Cultivation, Processing, and Trafficking in Colombia." Paper given at U.S. State Department Conference on Colombia, November 9, 1981, p. 6.

14. Premo, "U.S.-Colombian Relations . . . ," p. 9.

15. *Latin America   Weekly Report* (London), February 19, 1982.

16. Premo, "U.S.-Colombian Relations . . . ," pp. 13–14.

17. Premo, "U.S.-Colombian Relations . . . ," p. 16.

18. *El Espectador* (Bogotá), October 11, 1981.

19. *El Espectador* (Bogotá), January 31, 1982.

20. Francois J. Lombard, *The Foreign Investment Screening Process in LDCs: The Case of Colombia 1967–1975* (Boulder, Colo.: Westview Press, 1979), p. 124.

21. *El Espectador* (Bogotá), May 27, 1981.

22. David Morawetz, *Why the Emperor's New Clothes Are Not Made in Colombia* (New York: Oxford University Press, 1981), p. 57.

23. Confidential interview, U.S. diplomat, April 9, 1981.

24. Response to question, after lecture, at Centro Colombo-Americano, Bogotá, December 1, 1980.

25. *El Espectador* (Bogotá), May 29, 1981.

26. *El Tiempo* (Bogotá), April 9, 1981.

7

Conclusions and Prognosis

The preceding chapters have shown that Colombia is a complex country, because of regionalism, social class, political history, economic model, and random personal factors as well as others. Indeed, it is not unusual for the foreign observer to discover that first impressions (and the "easy" solutions that might come with them) are muddied by acquiring more information, rather than reinforced by that data-collecting experience. Hence liberal democratic pluralists, Marxists, and those looking for a corporate society and/or state will find some information that reinforces their ideological biases and much more that does not.

One might even argue that Colombia is the most complex, or at least one of the most complex, countries of Latin America. Clearly Cuba in 1959, Chile in 1970, and Nicaragua in 1979 were much simpler countries than Colombia is today. Neither has Colombia had a nationalist revolution such as that in Mexico or even that of Vargas in Brazil. In short, other countries of Latin America are not very good models for the Colombian future, nor is Colombia a good model for them.

While the purpose of this chapter is not to review all of the complexities of the country, there are two major goals. The first is to summarize—at a higher level of generality—the "Colombian model." The second is to consider various possibilities for the future.

CONCLUSIONS: THE COLOMBIAN MODEL

It is much easier to say what the Colombian model is *not* than to be affirmative (save in a retrospective fashion). The Colombian polity is *not* a liberal democracy, even though there are periodic elections and since 1974 there has been no electoral restraint, as there was in the National Front period. Yet Article 120 still prevents the president from choosing a cabinet and bureaucracy completely according to his preferences. Likewise, the Colombian polity is *not* characterized by interest-group pluralism. While perhaps, comparatively speaking, the right of the government to use *personería jurídica* is not exercised to the extent it is other Latin American countries, I have shown that it is used, particularly with labor and the *campesinos.* Occasionally the withdrawal of legal personality is a threat to other groups.

Colombia politically is *not* a dictatorship with *continuismo* (changing the constitution so that the dictator can stay in power) or *imposición* (the dictator imposing his hand-picked successor). But, although the Colombian president is legally prohibited from taking part in the election of his successor, his influence does play a role in the choice of the candidate of his party. Indeed, it has been argued that there is party, although no personal, *continuismo.* And, to take the argument one step further, one might argue that the National Front was a constitutional exercise in the *continuismo* of the two traditional parties. Neither is Colombia a dictatorship in which personal liberties are denied, such as Chile or Argentina today. But the *estatuto de seguridad* did make the executive branch—and the military—more of a force in day-to-day life than at any time since 1958, and both Colombian critics and Amnesty International have written about the violation of human rights.[1]

Economically Colombia is *not* a liberal-capitalist state in which economic groups are separate from the government. Rather there are all kinds of formal and informal connections between the capitalist groups and the government. Nor is economic policy primarily of one economic school. Policy is *not* consistently of the "Chicago School," as perhaps Chile's comes close to being, although many policies of the López M. and Turbay governments were of monetarist tendencies. Nor was it ever as much of the "ECLA School" (the Economic Commission for Latin America, a group that saw import substitution industrialization as a solution to Latin America's problems) as were many other Latin American countries. Lastly, economic policy is *not* socialist or state capitalist like that of Cuba or Nicaragua (the latter to a lesser degree at this writing). Rather, economic policy tends to be a combination of all of these, with state ownership of some industries, MNC ownership of others, and private ownership of still others. While this might sound like the Brazilian "tripé,"[2] one should hasten to reiterate that the Colombian state is the weakest of the three in this relationship.

In short, the Colombian model is an eclectic one that is neither democratic nor dictatorial in political terms[3] nor capitalist, state capitalist, or socialist in economic ones. Some see this as a great strength of the country in the last twenty years. As the economic journal *Estrategia económica y financiera* (headed by Rodrigo Botero, first minister of *hacienda* of the López government) stated at the end of 1980,

> Economic policy, which has been gaining certain intellectual consensus in the country, is an eclectic mixture of market economics and of state interventionism in which elements of import substitution coexist with elements of export promotion; protectionism, with international competition; the stimulation of a vigorous private sector, with the deliberate action of the state as an industrial mover and promoter in determined fields; relative financial liberty internally, with exchange controls; stimuli to foreign private investment, with strict limits to its behavior; a prudent monetary and fiscal management, with deliberate efforts to modify the productive structure of the country. . . . In the political aspect, the model has produced legitimacy in the exercise of government; ordered, predictable, and periodic transfer of power; and clear limitations to authority. This in turn has given sufficient continuity to economic and social policy in order to gain experience, develop institutions, and to get going long-term programs and projects.[4]

To support these arguments, *Estrategia* presented data that showed that during the period 1950 to 1980 GDP per capita was growing, infant mortality was going down, life expectancy and literacy were increasing, and the population growth rate went down.

Others would disagree. They maintain that the state apparatus is one of the weakest in Latin America, that MNCs have been allowed to run many key parts of the economy (including Cerrejón coal) and have made huge profits, that economic policy has suffered from the lack of continuity, and that democratic power is but a facade behind which the military really governs. Some would even doubt the reliability of the data on which the *Estrategia* argument is made. They would argue (counterfactually) that, while there has been economic progress in the last twenty years, there would have been more if (1) the role of the state had been greater, (2) there had been a socialist economy, or (3) there had been no protective tariffs and if Colombian industry had competed with international business. While there might be a certain merit to any or all of the three arguments (or indeed others along similar counterfactual lines that I have not mentioned), the point is that empirically neither the *Estrategia* people nor their critics can prove that they are right. To do so, one logically would have to recreate history and try another policy—something possible in physics, perhaps, but not in social sciences.

Further, one of the writers at *Estrategia* told me that the Colombian model as described above does not have predictable power: If there is a possibility of developing a new economic good, this model cannot be used to predict if such will be done by the government, Colombian capitalists, MNCs, or some combination of the three. As the *Estrategia* writer told me, "You just have to wait and see."[5] In short, while this "bureaucratic" or "interest group" model might be useful in describing the Colombian system, it has little explanatory power (except in a tautological fashion) and no predictive power.

PROSPECTS FOR THE FUTURE

Futurology is always somewhat hazardous (unless an author couches the predictions in such long-term statements that he or she is long forgotten when they are proved to be false). One difficulty in making predictions is the great number of variables; others are the random factors and the effects of the predictions themselves on the outcomes. A somewhat random factor has been seen in Colombia recently: ten years ago, who would have predicted the economic, political, and social effects of the drug trade? Another such "random" thing in the next decade might be border conflict with Venezuela or the discovery of new economic resources. Secondly, if Colombian policy makers are concerned with the problems highlighted in this work, they might take action that would change the assumptions on which predictions are made. Yet "what the future holds" is of such interest that I would be remiss if some predictions were not made.

Concern for this Colombian future was shown at a U.S. State Department Conference on Colombia, held in November 1981. The participants were asked to address their remarks, in general, to the question of Colombia in the future. Three alternatives were given: "apocalypse" (defined as leftist civil war, perhaps leading to a "Cuba"); "Southern Cone" (a military dictatorship like Argentina, Uruguay, or Chile); or "muddling through" (a continued fairly good performance, with elections and the eclecticism described in the previous section). Most of the participants agreed on the last of the three alternatives.

Yet asking academic participants for one of these three "bottom lines" was a rather simplistic task. I argue that, while at the present "muddling through" seems to be the most likely prognosis, much depends on the state of the economy and on factors outside of Colombia. In this section I will show that "muddling through" contains several different variants with meaningful differences.

Apocalypse

At least since the Cuban revolution, Colombians (and North American advisers) have been concerned that a Castro-like movement would sweep through the Andes and replace, among others, the Colombian political elite. That such has not occurred in three decades leads some to conclude that there is no danger, although recent cases in Nicaragua and El Salvador (perceived to be very similar to the Cuban case) have brought the specter to center stage once again.

Clearly a potential for violent revolution does exist—at least if one assumes, as I do, that such revolutions come from maldistribution of the wealth of societies. Evidence suggests that Colombia has one of the most inequitable distributions of wealth in Latin America, which, other things being equal, would give the country a high potential for civil war and apocalypse. (It should be clear that this would be a different Revelation for the upper and middle groups than for the great majority of the poor people, at least in economic terms.) Yet other things, including the following, are not equal.

Regionalism makes it difficult for there to be a national popular movement behind one, or even a few, revolutionary leaders. In all of Colombian history, the Catholic church and the two traditional political parties—whatever their defects—have been the only nationwide organizations outside of the government. Given the regional differences discussed in Chapter 1, it is difficult to imagine most Colombian poor people following a revolutionary leader from Antioquia—or much less, a *costeño*. (Jaime Bateman, leader of the M-19, is the latter.) Yet to the degree that regional differences continue to disappear, this impediment may become less important.

Unlike the cases of several Central American nations, the church hierarchy and the parish priests have not supported revolutionary movements. Liberation Theology, while it certainly exists in the Colombian church, is not dominant. If, however, growing numbers of priests were to support a leftist movement, the probability of its success would be greatly enhanced.

There is no obvious target for a leftist movement in Colombia. Of course, there is the *oligarquía*, and the poor in the cities (where they increasingly are) can see the conspicuous consumption of the rich; in many cases, the poor work for those who have consumer durables far beyond those of the mythical U.S. "middle class." The point is that, up to now, there has been no one single symbol: no Batista, no Somoza, not even a Duarte. In Colombian "democracy" there is always the theoretical possibility that the poor could get together and win elections. While this possibility is more theoretical than real, it does defuse the revolutionary potential.

Some would argue that the Colombian masses are weary of violence, already having had twenty years of it. Besides this weariness there are the traditional party ties, perhaps reinforced by *La Violencia*. Even though these ascriptive loyalties seem to be dying out, their interment is very premature at this point.

If there should be incipient leftist movements (as of course there already are—at least four of them, as described in Chapter 4) the Colombian elite would cry "Cuba," and the U.S. government would rush to aid them. Such has already occurred: In March 1981, when captured M-19 rebels said they had been trained in Cuba and Panama, the Turbay government hastened to end diplomatic relations with the socialist island (but not with Panama). Secretary of State Haig, in his early 1982 testimony in the U.S. Congress, mentioned Colombia as one of the countries threatened by Cuba and the Soviet Union. As U.S. private investment is greater in Colombia than in El Salvador and as Colombia is nearer to Venezuelan oil, the Panama Canal, and the sea lanes frequently mentioned by U.S. officials, one might surmise that any serious apocalyptic threat would be met by massive U.S. government intervention. (I might add—although I have never visited Southeast Asia—that Colombia's topography would make Vietnam seem easy.)

For these reasons, it is my opinion that a successful leftist guerrilla movement in Colombia is improbable in the current world system. However, so long as the majority of Colombians live without proper nutrition, decent housing, and hope for the future, the possibility remains.

There is, of course, a particularly Colombian version of apocalypse— that of *La Violencia*. During at least the last ten years of the National Front, U.S. scholars wrote about the possibility of a return to *La Violencia* after the front. This also seems unlikely: No longer are the majority of Colombians living in the countryside, and perhaps no longer do the majority identify with one of the political parties.

Southern Cone

The Southern Cone scenario is that of military dictatorship along the lines of Chile, Argentina, Uruguay, or Brazil, that is, what recently has been called "bureaucratic authoritarianism."[6] Research on the Southern Cone countries demonstrates that such government by the military establishment (as opposed to personal dictatorship by a particular general) comes in either the situation of stagnation of import substitution and/ or the growth of populist movements. When the "bottlenecks" of ISI are reached or when lower-class groups are organized, the military steps in to maintain a stability that is not possible when democratic leaders give too much to the lower classes.

It might be argued that if such prerequisites are necessary bureaucratic authoritarianism is not likely in Colombia for two reasons. The first is that Colombia was late in accepting ISI (thus bringing in industry that was more capital intensive and less dependent on organized labor) and, further, turned away from ISI as the primary economic goal through Law 444 of 1967. Second, populist movements have never been important in Colombia.[7] The latter is simply because the lower classes (on whom populism would be based) have always been split between the two traditional parties. The most successful populist movement in Colombian history was Gustavo Rojas Pinilla's ANAPO, which many still believe did win the 1970 presidential election. Yet that was populism during the "artificial" years of the National Front, when Liberals in 1970 had to vote for a Conservative for president or for no one at all. We will never know how Rojas would have done after the National Front: his bad health caused him to pass the mantle on to his daughter.

Yet I have just argued in the previous section that a repeat of *La Violencia* is not likely because of the weakening of those traditional psychological ties to the two parties. If that is correct, movements based on the lower classes might be more possible in the future. If those movements should become as strong as the Unidad Popular in Chile or if they should be perceived to be as great a threat as the Tupamaros in Uruguay or the leftist groups in Brazil in early 1964, then at that point a Colombian version of bureaucratic authoritarianism would be a distinct possibility. It is true that the Colombian military has little experience in governing, that military officers are not held in high esteem by political leaders, and that the military is divided between "hard-liners" who support the *estatuto de seguridad* and "soft-liners" who think that economic problems lie behind subversion. But none of those three characteristics is greatly different from that of the Chilean or Uruguayan military ten short years ago.

One might even argue that Colombia had one of the first bureaucratic authoritarian experiences in Latin America—the government of Rojas Pinilla from 1953 to 1957. Clearly that government, in retrospect, did not fit the definition simply because Rojas tried to keep power for himself rather than allowing another general to follow him. Yet popular mobilization (albeit primarily in the form of civil war between the two parties) was the major reason for the Rojas coup. I therefore think that military takeover is a real possibility should there be popular mobilization in a future Colombia. If that mobilization were in the form of a revolutionary movement, the present administration in Washington, at least, would see "Southern Cone" as preferable to "apocalypse."

"Muddling Through"

Perhaps the greatest possibility, simply because of inertia, would be that of eclectic "muddling through." In this scenario, nothing would dramatically change from the system described in Chapter 4. The same basic model would continue, with fine tuning depending on whether, for example, foreign exchange were abundant or scarce. (It is of note in this connection that the López government's lowering of tariffs during high coffee prices, so as to avoid inflation, was not a new strategy. Similar strategies previously had been followed during other coffee bonanzas.)[8] Elections would continue between the two traditional parties, interest groups would continue to have their current bias, and the right of *personería jurídica* would be used selectively.

Yet it is my opinion that "muddling through" is a broad category that obscures different alternatives that might have great effects on millions of Colombians. I will, for purposes of brevity, discuss the two polar cases of "muddling through."

The most conservative version of "muddling through" would be one not unlike the Turbay administration, although it would not necessarily have to have as much patronage politics as those years did. The conservative version would be characterized by even more dependence on the "market place" forces of the international political economy. Colombian industry would be allowed to disappear if it could not compete internationally and would not be protected. When jobs were lost, "Chicago School" followers would argue that "comparative advantage" allows for the greatest benefit for the greater number of Colombians. Coffee, coal, nickel, and a few other products would be sent out of the country with little or no value added, while manufactured consumer goods would be imported. The consumer goods might be less expensive, because of economies of scale and other factors, than they are now. However, in a microeconomic sense, millions might be unemployed or underemployed. The government elite (if it were an intelligent one) would subsidize those millions so as to maintain its own stability.

The most liberal version of "muddling through" would be rather more nationalist than recent Colombian governments. Multinational corporations would be closely watched, so as to make certain that exorbitant profits were not legally or illegally taken from the country. The large Colombian financial groups and the *oligarquía* would be taxed and controlled so that there could be some redistribution of wealth. Tariff barriers would be maintained to some degree, so as to protect Colombian industry and to keep unemployment down. Manufacturing growth would be a key goal, because that development would employ more people, and Colombian products would have more value added. (It is of note that, at this writing, cocaine is the one Colombian export with most value added—not legal manufactures). In the case of the new richness of Colombian coal, there would be pressure to renegotiate the contract with Exxon so that transfer pricing could better be controlled and so that the Colombian government would play a more active role in coal production. The coal money would be "sown" as the Venezuelans once talked of "sowing the petroleum"—that is, using the earnings to build Colombian industry and infrastructure. Coal liquefaction and gasification would be emphasized so that the national riches could be exported with value added. The nationalism of this version of "muddling through" might also bring a national self-confidence, something sorely lacking today among the government elite (but interestingly enough, not among the "informal sector"[9] or the drug runners[10]).

Either version of "muddling through"—or the various gradations in between the two extremes—might include a realigning of Colombian political parties. This could come through (1) the two parties consistently taking ideological positions that would be twentieth-century reflections of their nineteenth-century names; (2) new political parties taking different ideological positions; or (3) more or less stable coalitions between the progressives in both parties, on the one hand, and the more conservative groups, on the other. At this writing, the last of the three seems most likely, although the first two alternatives would make voter rationality more of a possibility.

FINAL WORDS

It is my opinion that, in the final analysis, economic conditions will be paramount in determining the future course of Colombian politics and society. Dependency will continue: the question will be how to use dependency to the good of the country. If the Colombian economy does well, as it has in the decades until 1979, there will be little popular pressure for change. If, on the other hand, the recession coming from outside of the country continues or worsens, there will be calls for change. How radical these demands are will depend, in good part, on how bad the economic conditions are.

But no matter which route is taken, Colombia will remain unique when the twenty-first century arrives. The country has a historical claim to uniqueness and should be allowed by all to develop along its own course.

NOTES

1. Comité Permanente por la Defensa de los Derechos Humanos, *Represión y Tortura en Colombia* (Bogotá: Fondo Editorial Suramérica, 1980).

2. Peter Evans, *Dependent Development: The Alliance of Multinational, State, and Local Capital in Brazil* (Princeton: Princeton University Press, 1979), *passim*.

3. Some recent, and potentially very valuable, research has focused on the "consociational" nature of Colombian democracy, that is, a political system in which the elites make deliberate decisions, sometimes antimajoritarian, to

bring stability to a badly divided society. See Robert H. Dix, "Consociational Democracy: The Case of Colombia," *Comparative Politics*, 12 (1980): 303–321 and Jonathan Hartlyn, "Consociational Politics in Colombia: Confrontation and Accommodation in Comparative Perspective," Ph.D. dissertation, Yale University, 1981.

4. "Observaciones acerca del modelo colombiano de desarrollo 1958–1980," *Estrategia económica y financiera*, 38 (Octubre 1980): 3, 9–10.

5. Confidential interview, *Estrategia* journalist, April 20, 1981.

6. See, among others, David Collier, ed., *The New Authoritarianism in Latin America* (Princeton: Princeton University Press, 1979).

7. This topic is addressed in two excellent (but greatly different) recent pieces. See J. Mark Ruhl, "An Alternative to the Bureaucratic-Authoritarian Regime: The Case of Colombian Modernization," *Inter-American Economic Affairs*, 35, no. 2 (1981): 43–69; and Jonathan Hartlyn, "The Impact of a Country's Pre-Industrial Structure and the International System on Political Regime Type: A Case Study of Colombia," Paper presented at the 23rd Annual International Studies Association Convention, Cincinnati, 1982.

8. Alfredo Fuentes Hernández and Ricardo Villaveces Pardo, "La Liberación Actual de Importaciones y su Perspectiva Histórica," *Coyuntura Económica*, 6 (Junio 1976): 87–98.

9. This insight came from a series of conversations in the first half of 1981 with William and Christina Tucker, both of whom work for charitable organizations that work with the "informal sector" (Bill) or poor people in general (Chris).

10. Confidential interview, employee of U.S. government, June 6, 1981.

Bibliography

Arciniegas, Germán. *Biografía del Caribe*. Buenos Aires: Editorial Sudamericana, 1963.

———. *The State of Latin America*. Translated by Harriet de Onis. New York: Alfred A. Knopf, 1952.

Atlas Básico de Colombia. Bogotá: Instituto Geográfico "Agustín Codazzi," 1980.

Bagley, Bruce Michael. "Beyond the National Front: State and Society in Contemporary Colombia." Paper presented at the U.S. State Department Conference on Colombia, Washington, D.C., November 9, 1981.

———. "Political Power, Public Policy and the State in Colombia: Case Studies of the Urban and Agrarian Reforms during the National Front, 1958–1974." Ph.D. dissertation, Political Science, University of California, Los Angeles, 1979.

Bernal, Segundo. "Las regiones colombianas y sus estructuras espaciales (resumen)." *Revista Mensual de Estadística* 346 (1980): 7–62.

Berry, R. Albert. "Colombia's Economic Situation and Prospects." Paper presented at the U.S. State Department Conference on Colombia, Washington, D.C., November 9, 1981.

———, and Soligo, Ronald. "The Distribution of Income in Colombia: An Overview," in R. Albert Berry and Ronald Soligo (eds.) *Economic Policy and Income Distribution in Colombia*. Boulder, Colo.: Westview Press, 1980.

Bushnell, David. "Colombia," in Harold Eugene Davis, Larman C. Wilson, and others, *Latin American Foreign Politics: An Analysis*. Baltimore: The Johns Hopkins University Press, 1975, 401–418.

Collier, David (ed.). *The New Authoritarianism in Latin America*. Princeton: Princeton University Press, 1979.

Colmenares, Germán. *Partidos Políticos y Clases Sociales*. Bogotá: Ediciones Universidad de los Andes, 1968.

Comité Permanente por la Defensa de los Derechos Humanos. *Represión y Tortura en Colombia*. Bogotá: Fondo Editorial Suramérica, 1980.

Confidential interview, CARBOCOL official, June 4, 1981.

Confidential interview, former ECOPETROL official, Bogotá, April 24, 1981.

149

Confidential interview, former minister of economic development, Bogotá, April 10, 1981.

Confidential interview, former minister of *hacienda*, Bogotá, April 20, 1981.

Confidential interview, journalist of *Estrategia económica y financiera*, Bogotá, April 20, 1981.

Confidential interview, U.S. diplomat, Bogotá, April 9, 1981.

Confidential interview, U.S. government employee, Bogotá, June 6, 1981.

Craig, Richard B. "Domestic Implications of Illicit Drug Cultivation, Processing, and Trafficking in Colombia." Paper presented at the U.S. State Department Conference on Colombia, Washington, D.C., November 9, 1981.

Diaz-Alejandro, Carlos F. *Foreign Trade Regimes and Economic Development: Colombia*. New York: National Bureau of Economic Research, 1976.

División de Estudios Económicos, DANE. "El comercio exterior Colombiano en 1979." *Revista Mensual de Estadística* 348 (Julio 1980): 31–51.

Dix, Robert H. *Colombia: The Political Dimensions of Change*. New Haven: Yale University Press, 1967.

———. "Consociational Democracy: The Case of Colombia." *Comparative Politics* 12 (1980): 303–321.

El Espectador (Bogotá), May 27, 1981; May 29, 1981; October 11, 1981; November 8, 1981; January 31, 1982; and March 14, 1982.

Evans, Peter. *Dependent Development: The Alliance of Multinational, State, and Local Capital in Brazil*. Princeton: Princeton University Press, 1979.

Fagg, John Edwin. *Latin America: A General History*. New York: Macmillan, 1963.

Fals Borda, Orlando. *Suversión y Cambio Social*. Bogotá: Ediciones Tercer Mundo, 1968.

Fluharty, Vernon Lee. *Dance of the Millions: Military Rule and the Social Revolution in Colombia 1930–1956*. 2nd ed. Pittsburgh: University of Pittsburgh Press, 1966.

Fuentes Hernández, Alfredo, and Villaveces Pardo, Ricardo. "La Liberación Actual de Importaciones y su Perspectiva Histórica." *Coyuntura Económica* 6 (Junio 1976): 87–98.

Galán, Luis Carlos. "El nuevo liberalismo." *El Tiempo* (Bogotá), June 8, 1981.

Gil, Federico. *Latin American–United States Relations*. New York: Harcourt Brace Jovanovich, 1971.

Gillis, Malcolm, and McLure, Jr., Charles E. "The 1974 Colombian Tax Reform and Income Distribution," in R. Albert Berry and Ronald Soligo (eds.) *Economic Policy and Income Distribution in Colombia*. Boulder, Colo.: Westview Press, 1980.

Guzmán Campos, Germán; Fals Borda, Orlando; and Umaña Luna, Eduardo. *La Violencia en Colombia*. 2 vols. Bogotá: Ediciones Tercer Mundo, 1962, 1964.

Harkness, Shirley, and Pinzón de Lewin, Patricia. "Women, the Vote, and the Party in the Politics of the Colombian National Front." *Journal of Interamerican Studies and World Affairs* 17 (1975): 439–463.

Hartlyn, Jonathan. "Consociational Politics in Colombia: Confrontation and

Accommodation in Comparative Perspective." Ph.D. dissertation, Political Science, Yale University, 1981.

_____. "The Impact of a Country's Pre-Industrial Structure and the International System on Political Regime Type: A Case Study of Colombia." Paper presented at the 23rd Annual International Studies Association Convention, Cincinnati, 1982.

_____. "Interest Groups and Political Conflict in Colombia: A Retrospective and Prospective View." Paper presented at the U.S. State Department Conference on Colombia, Washington, D.C., November 9, 1981.

Havens, A. Eugene; Flinn, William L.; and Lastarria-Cornhill, Susana. "Agrarian Reform and the National Front: A Class Analysis," in R. Albert Berry, Ronald G. Hellman, and Mauricio Solaún (eds.) *Politics of Compromise: Coalition Government in Colombia.* New Brunswick, N.J.: Transaction Books, 1980, 341–379.

Henao, Jesús María; and Arrubla, Gerardo. *Historia de Colombia.* 8th ed. Bogotá: Talleres Editoriales de la Librería Voluntad, 1967.

Hoskin, Gary. "The Colombian Political Party System: Electoral Domination and System Instability." Paper presented at the U.S. State Department Conference on Colombia, Washington, D.C., November 9, 1981.

International Colombia Resources Corporation. "Commercial Declaration." July 1, 1980.

Jaramillo Uribe, Jaime. "Etapas y Sentido de la Historia de Colombia," in Mario Arrubla, et al. *Colombia Hoy.* Bogotá: Siglo Veintiuno Editores, 1980, 15–51.

Kline, Harvey F. "The Coal of 'El Cerrejón': An Historical Analysis of Major Colombian Policy Decisions and MNC Activities." *Inter-American Economic Affairs* 35 (Winter 1981): 69–90.

_____. "The Cohesion of Political Parties in the Colombian Congress: A Case Study of the 1968 Session." Ph.D. dissertation, Government, University of Texas, 1970.

_____. *Energy Policy and the Colombian Elite: A Synthesis and Interpretation.* Occasional Paper no. 4, The Center for Hemispheric Studies. Washington, D.C.: American Enterprise Institute, 1982.

_____. *Exxon and Colombian Coal: An Analysis of the North Cerrejón Debates.* Occasional Papers Series no. 14. Amherst: Program in Latin American Studies, University of Massachusetts at Amherst, 1982.

_____. "The National Front: Historical Perspective and Overview," in R. Albert Berry, Ronald G. Hellman, and Mauricio Solaún (eds.) *Politics of Compromise: Coalition Government in Colombia.* New Brunswick, N.J.: Transaction Books, 1980, 59–83.

_____. "Selección de Candidatos," in Gary Hoskin et al. *Estudio del Comportamiento en Colombia.* Bogotá: Editorial Universidad de los Andes, 1975, 169–206.

Latin America Weekly Report (London), November 13, 1981; January 8, 1982; February 19, 1982.

Leal Buitrago, Francisco. "Social Classes, International Trade and Foreign Capital in Colombia: An Attempt at Historical Interpretation of the Formation of the State, 1819–1935." Ph.D. dissertation, Development, University of Wisconsin, 1974.

Levine, Daniel H. *Religion and Politics in Latin America: The Catholic Church in Venezuela and Colombia*. Princeton: Princeton University Press, 1981.

Lleras Camargo, Alberto. *Sus Mejores Páginas*. Bogotá: n.p., n.d.

Lombard, Francois J. *The Foreign Investment Screening Process in LDCs: The Case of Colombia, 1967–1975*. Boulder, Colo.: Westview Press, 1979.

López de Rodríguez, Cecilia, and León de Leal, Magdalena. "El Trabajo de la Mujer," in Magdalena León de Leal (ed.) *La Mujer y el Desarrollo en Colombia*. Bogotá: ACEP, 1977, 183–228.

Losada, Rodrigo. "Electoral Participation," in R. Albert Berry, Ronald G. Hellman, and Mauricio Solaún (eds.) *Politics of Compromise: Coalition Government in Colombia*. New Brunswick, N.J.: Transaction Books, 1980, 87–104.

Martz, John D. *Colombia: A Contemporary Political Survey*. Chapel Hill: University of North Carolina Press, 1962.

McGreevey, William Paul. "Population Policy under the National Front," in R. Albert Berry, Ronald G. Hellman, and Mauricio Solaún (eds.) *Politics of Compromise: Coalition Government in Colombia*. New Brunswick, N.J.: Transaction Books, 1980, 413–432.

Ministerio de Minas y Energía. *Bases para un plan energético nacional*. Bogotá: n.p., 1977.

Morawetz, David. *Why the Emperor's New Clothes Are Not Made in Colombia*. New York: Oxford University Press, 1981.

"Observaciones acerca del modelo colombiano de desarrollo 1958–1980." *Estrategia económica y financiera* 38 (Octubre 1980): 5–11.

Oquist, Paul. *Violence, Conflict, and Politics in Colombia*. New York: Academic Press, 1980.

Payne, James L. "The Oligarchy Muddle." *World Politics* 20 (1968): 439–453.

_____. *Patterns of Conflict in Colombia*. New Haven: Yale University Press, 1968.

Premo, Daniel L. "The Armed Forces and Colombian Politics: In Search of a Mission." Chestertown, Md.: Washington College, 1981. (Mimeographed.)

_____. "U.S.-Colombian Relations: A Contemporary Perspective." Chestertown, Md.: Washington College, 1981. (Mimeographed.)

Rippy, J. Fred. *The Capitalists and Colombia*. New York: Vanguard Press, 1931.

Rivera Ortiz, Angel Israel. "The Politics of Development Planning in Colombia." Ph.D. dissertation, Political Science, State University of New York at Buffalo, 1976.

Ruhl, J. Mark. "An Alternative to the Bureaucratic-Authoritarian Regime: The Case of Colombian Modernization." *Inter-American Economic Affairs* 35 (1981): 43–69.

_____. "Civil-Military Relations in Colombia: A Societal Explanation." *Journal of Interamerican Studies and World Affairs* 23 (1981): 123–146.

_____. *Colombia: Armed Forces and Society*. Foreign and Comparative Studies, Latin American Series. Syracuse, N.Y.: 1980.

Santa, Eduardo. *Sociología Política de Colombia*. Bogotá: Ediciones Tercer Mundo, 1964.

Schmidt, Steffen W. "Women in Colombia: Attitudes and Future Perspectives in the Political System." *Journal of Interamerican Studies and World Affairs* 17 (1975): 465–489.

Sharpless, Richard E. *Gaitán of Colombia: A Political Biography.* Pittsburgh: University of Pittsburgh Press, 1978.

Sheahan, John. *Aspects of Planning and Development in Colombia.* Technical Paper Series no. 10. Austin, Tex.: The Institute of Latin American Studies, 1977.

Silva Colmenares, Julio. *Los Verdaderos Dueños del País.* Bogotá: Fondo Editorial Suramérica, 1977.

Simons, Marlise. "Storyteller with Bent for Revolution: Gabriel García Márquez." *New York Times.* October 22, 1982, A10.

Subcommittee on American Republics Affairs, Committee on Foreign Relations, U.S. Senate. *Survey of the Alliance for Progress, Colombia—A Case History of U.S. Aid.* Washington, D.C.: Government Printing Office, 1969.

El Tiempo (Bogotá), April 9, 1981.

Urrutia, Miguel. *The Development of the Colombian Labor Movement.* New Haven: Yale University Press, 1969.

————. "Diversidad ideológica e integración Andina." *Coyuntura Económica* 10 (1980): 187–203.

Villegas, Jorge. *Petróleo, Oligarquía e Imperio.* Bogotá: Ediciones E.S.E., 1969.

Vinocur, John. "García Márquez Wins Nobel; Radical Colombian Novelist." *New York Times.* October 22, 1982, A1.

World Bank. *World Development Report 1981.* Washington, D.C.: World Bank, 1981.

Wilde, Alexander W. "Conservations among Gentlemen: Oligarchical Democracy in Colombia," in Juan J. Linz and Alfred Stepan (eds.) *The Breakdown of Democratic Regimes: Latin America.* Baltimore: The Johns Hopkins University Press, 1978, 28–81.

Williams, Miles Wendell. "El Frente Nacional: Colombia's Experiment in Controlled Democracy." Ph.D. dissertation, Political Science, Vanderbilt University, 1972.

Abbreviations

ACOPI	Asociación Colombiana de Pequeños Industriales (Colombian Association of Small Industrialists)
ADPOSTAL	Administración Postal Nacional (National Postal Administration)
AID	Agency for International Development
ANAPO	Alianza Nacional Popular (National Popular Alliance)
ANAPO-FUP	Alianza Nacional Popular-Frente Unido del Pueblo (National Popular Alliance-Peoples United Front)
ANDI	Asociación Nacional de Industriales (National Association of Industrialists)
ANIF	Asociación Nacional de Instituciones Financieras (National Association of Financial Institutions)
ANUC	Asociación Nacional de Usuarios Campesinos (National Association of Peasants)
ASOBANCARIA	Asociación Bancaria de Colombia (Colombian Bankers Association)
CAMACOL	Cámara Colombiana de Construcción (Colombian Chamber of Construction)
CARBOCOL	Carbones de Colombia (Colombian Coal Company)
CAT	*certificado de abono tributario* (a general tax-credit certificate)
CGT	Confederación General de Trabajo (General Confederation of Workers)
COLCIENCIAS	Fondo Colombiano de Investigaciones Científicas y Proyectos Especiales (Colombian Fund for Scientific Investigations and Special Projects)

155

COLCULTURA	Instituto Colombiana de Cultura (Colombian Institute of Culture)
COLDEPORTES	Instituto Colombiano de la Juventud y el Deporte (Colombian Institute of Youth and Sport)
COLPUERTOS	Empresa Puertos de Colombia (Colombian Port Enterprise)
CONFECAMARAS	Confederación Colombiana de Cámaras de Comercio (Colombian Confederation of Chambers of Commerce)
CONPES	Concejo Nacional de Política Económica y Social (National Council of Economic & Social Policy)
CSTC	Confederación Sindical de Trabajadores de Colombia (Syndical [or Union] Confederation of Colombian Workers)
CTC	Confederación de Trabajadores Colombianos (Confederation of Colombian Workers)
DNP	Departamento Nacional de Planeación (National Planning Department)
ECLA	Economic Commission for Latin America
ECOMINAS	Empresa Colombiana de Minas (Colombian Mining Enterprise)
ECOPETROL	Empresa Colombiana de Petróleos (Colombian Petroleum Enterprise)
ELN	Ejército de Liberación Nacional (National Liberation Army)
EPL	Ejército Popular de Liberación (People's Liberation Army)
FARC	Fuerzas Armadas Revolucionarias Colombianas (Revolutionary Armed Forces of Colombia)
FASECOLDA	Unión de Aseguradores Colombianos (Union of Colombian Insurance Companies)
FEDECAFE	Federación Nacional de Cafeteros (National Federation of Coffee Growers)
FEDEGAN	Federación Nacional de Ganaderos (National Federation of Livestock Raisers)
FEDEMETAL	Federación Colombiana de Industrias Metalúrgicas (Colombian Federation of Metallurgical Industries)
FENALCO	Federación Nacional de Comerciantes (National Federation of Merchants)
FFCC	Ferrocarriles Nacionales de Colombia (National Railroads of Colombia)

GDP	gross domestic product
HIMAT	Instituto Colombiano de Hidrología, Meterología, y Adecuación de Tierras (Colombian Institute of Hydrology, Meteorology, and Land Improvement)
ICBF	Instituto Colombiano de Bienestar Familiar (Colombian Institute of Family Welfare)
ICEL	Instituto Colombiano de Energía Eléctrica (Colombian Institute of Electric Energy)
ICFES	Instituto Colombiano para el Fomento de la Educación Superior (Colombian Institute for the Promotion of Higher Education)
ICSS	Instituto Colombiano de los Seguros Sociales (Colombian Institute of Social Security)
ICT	Instituto de Crédito Territorial (Institute of Land Credit)
IDB	Inter-American Development Bank
IFI	Instituto de Fomento Industrial (Industrial Promotion Institute)
IMF	International Monetary Fund
INCOMEX	Instituto Colombiano de Comercio Exterior (Foreign Trade Institute)
INCORA	Instituto Colombiano de la Reforma Agraria (Colombian Agrarian Reform Institute)
INDERENA	Instituto de Desarrollo de Recursos Naturales Renovables y del Ambiente (Institute for the Development of Renewable Natural Resources and of the Environment)
INGEOMINAS	Instituto Nacional de Investigaciones Geológico-Mineras (National Institute of Geological Mining Investigations)
INRAVISION	Instituto Nacional de Radio y Televisión (National Institute of Radio and Television)
INTERCOR	International Colombia Resources Corporation
INTRA	Instituto Nacional de Transporte (National Institute of Transportation)
ISI	import substitution industrialization
LAFTA	Latin American Free Trade Association
MAS	Muerte a Secuestradores (Death to Kidnappers)
MNC	multinational corporation

M-19	Movimiento 19 de Abril (19th of April Movement)
MRL	Movimiento Revolucionario Liberal (Revolutionary Liberal Movement)
OAS	Organization of American States
OPEC	Organization of Petroleum Exporting Countries
PCC	Partido Comunista Colombiano (Colombian Communist party)
PRI	Partido Revolucionario Institutional (Revolutionary Institutional party)
PROEXPO	Fondo de Promoción de Exportaciones (Export Promotion Fund)
SAC	Sociedad de Agricultores de Colombia (Colombian Agricultural Society)
SENA	Servicio Nacional de Aprendizaje (National Apprenticeship Service)
SENDAS	Secretariado Nacional de Asistencia Social (National Secretariat of Social Assistance)
TELECOM	Empresa Nacional de Telecomunicaciones (National Telecommunications Enterprise)
UFCO	United Fruit Company
UN	United Nations
UPAC	Unidades de Poder Adquisitivo Constante (Units of Constant Buying Power)
UTC	Union de Trabajadores Colombianos (Union of Colombian Workers)

Index

ACOPI. *See* Colombian Association of Small Industrialists

ADPOSTAL. *See* National Postal Administration

Agency for International Development (AID), 91, 105, 108, 110, 122, 126, 128, 136

Agrarian Credit Bank (Caja Agraria), 70, 72

Agrarian reform, 21, 48, 84, 91, 126–127: Law 200 of 1936, 48; Law 135 of 1961, 104–105, 107; Law 1 of 1968, 107–108; *renta presuntiva*, 109–110; *See also* Colombian Agrarian Reform Institute

Agriculture, 1, 8, 15, 18, 101. *See also* Agrarian reform

AID. *See* Agency for International Development

Alliance for Progress, 91, 105, 125–128, 136

Alternativa (magazine), 25

Amazon River, 12–14, 75, 125

ANAPO. *See* National Popular Alliance

ANAPO-FUP. *See* National Popular Alliance–Peoples United Front

Andean Development Corporation, 128

Andean Multinational Enterprises, 129–130

Andean Pact, 105, 109, 128–131

Andes mountain region, 1, 3–4, 7, 24–25, 50

ANDI. *See* National Association of Industrialists

ANIF. *See* National Association of Financial Institutions

Andrade, Felio, 68

Antioquia, 32, 143

ANUC. *See* National Association of Peasants

Argentina, 134, 140, 142, 144

Article 120. *See* Constitutions, Reform of 1968

ASOBANCARIA. *See* Colombian Bankers Association

Banco de la República, 70, 72, 92: *ventanilla siniestra*, 115

Barrancabermeja refinery, 111–112

Barranquilla, 11–12, 91

Bateman, Jaime, 85, 143

Belalcázar, Sebastián de, 32

Benidorm Pact. *See* Frente Nacional

Betancur, Belisario, 57, 61, 73, 77: presidency of, 76, 78, 93

Blacks, 4, 9, 11–13, 32, 36

Bogotá, 3–4, 8, 25, 29, 32, 34, 39, 75, 84–85, 88, 91, 108, 116, 118: Bogotazo, 50, 125; Conference of, 125; Declaration of, 128

About the Book and Author

COLOMBIA
Portrait of Unity and Diversity
Harvey F. Kline

Colombia fits few of the patterns often associated with Latin America. Military coups are infrequent: There have been only four years of military government in this century. People are not all Indians, nor all coffee growers, nor all associated with the drug trade, nor all poverty stricken. Rather, they are diverse in ethnic background and socioeconomic strata.

Professor Kline discusses this heterogeneous country of 28 million people, looking first at its geography, population, and culture, and in more detail at its political history, which, he argues, weighs heavily on Colombian politics today. He then turns to an analysis of the contemporary political and economic systems of Colombia and considers the country's international relations, especially those with the United States, Venezuela, and Cuba. He concludes with an examination of the Colombian "model" and with projections of Colombia's future.

Harvey F. Kline is an associate professor in the Department of Political Science at the University of Massachusetts, Amherst. He has been a visiting professor at the Universidad de los Andes, Bogotá, Colombia.